TIGERS AND THE INTERNET

TIGERS AND THE INTERNET

STORY, SHAMANS, HISTORY

KIRA VAN DEUSEN

McGill-Queen's University Press
Montreal & Kingston • London • Chicago

ISBN 978-0-2280-1114-9 (cloth)
ISBN 978-0-2280-1353-2 (ePDF)
ISBN 978-0-2280-1354-9 (ePUB)

Legal deposit second quarter 2022
Bibliothèque nationale du Québec

Printed in Canada on acid-free paper that is 100% ancient forest free (100% post-consumer recycled), processed chlorine free

Funded by the Government of Canada | Financé par le gouvernement du Canada | Canada

We acknowledge the support of the Canada Council for the Arts.

Nous remercions le Conseil des arts du Canada de son soutien.

Library and Archives Canada Cataloguing in Publication

Title: Tigers and the Internet : story, shamans, history / Kira Van Deusen.

Names: Van Deusen, Kira, 1946- author.
Description: Includes bibliographical references and index.
Identifiers: Canadiana (print) 20210388471 | Canadiana (ebook) 20210388498 | ISBN 9780228011149 (cloth) | ISBN 9780228013532 (ePDF) | ISBN 9780228013549 (ePUB)
Subjects: LCSH: Udekhe (Asian people)—Russia (Federation)—Primorskiĭ kraĭ. | LCSH: Storytellers—Russia (Federation)—Primorskiĭ kraĭ. | LCSH: Tales—Russia (Federation)—Primorskiĭ kraĭ. | LCSH: Primorskiĭ kraĭ (Russia)—Social life and customs.
Classification: LCC DK759.U3 V36 2022 | DDC 305.894/1—dc23

This book was designed and typeset by studio oneonone in Minion 11/14

CONTENTS

ACKNOWLEDGMENTS

For many years I have known three women who became outstanding friends. Nadezhda Efimovna Kimonko is one who knows and does everything in both village and city. She introduced me to people and places. She gave endless explanations before, during, and after my being in Russia, starting in 1993.

Valentina Tunsianovna Kyalundzyuga has given friendship, teaching, spiritual understanding, books, and the sense of family for all that same time.

In the 1990s, Lyubov Passar told me about medicine and shamanism, which she knew well, and in 2020 and 2021 she gave me many things to read about culture and how things have changed – both before I arrived in the city of Khabarovsk.

More recently, Olesia Vladimirovna Shamshur, granddaughter of Valentina Tunsianovna, danced for us and played Udege musical instruments and had fun entertaining us.

Although she is no longer with us, I appreciate Yevdokia Batovna Kyalundzyuga for her knowledge of shamanism and great stories. On my most recent trip, I met her three daughters: Larissa Ilichna Kyalundzyuga, Nelli Ilichnia Andrea (born Kyalundzyuga), and Polina Ilinichna Sun. They shared memories of their mother, as well as laughter, and told me more about themselves. Larissa is a teacher, Nelli a hunter, and Polina a singer.

Great thanks to many shamans in these places: among the Udege I appreciate Vasiliy Dunkai, Adikhini Kyalundzyuga, Nadezhda Martynova (the last shaman in Krasny Yar before Dunkai).

We all appreciate Alex Frolenok for his excellent driving everywhere, and most of all for his superb photographs and good company.

Thanks to people who let us use their houses and a wonderful hot *banya* bath while in Gvasyugi village – also those who work at the school and museum. The confident children who play everywhere are a treat.

In Krasny Yar, we were given a comfortable place to stay, and help from the building's caretakers. People who gave us tea and delicious food as well as another *banya* were very helpful, as were people who took us around and explained things about the village.

Oksana Olegovna Zvidennaya was especially helpful in the village of Krasny Yar and afterwards. She also wrote to me when I came home, helping me to understand its politics.

Alexander Alexandrovich Kanchuga is also a good friend in Krasny Yar. I'll always remember him for smiles, memories, information on shamanism, translating, and another *banya* – a wonderful bath.

As we left Krasny Yar, people showed us a beautiful walk to the Bikin River, with tiger tracks on it. I've still never seen a tiger in the wild, although they are certainly there.

When we visited the Nanai territory, I met Victoria Donkan, Vera Onenko, Elena Kilye, Mingo Geiker, and Lindza Beldi. I also recalled a Buriat shaman Valentin Hagdaev, who lives in the middle of Siberia. Nadezhda Duvan, no longer with us, lived among the Ul'chi in the north.

In the city of Khabarovsk, I thank Nadezhda Kimonko again for her huge help and her co-workers for good company, tea, and cake. Thanks also to Gennadi Pavlishin for the use of some of his illustrations that I love so much.

In the United States, I thank Pavel Vasilievich Sulyandziga for helping me better understand the politics and culture of Indigenous life, and for sharing a poem. In turn he wishes to thank the kind people in the United States for making him and his family welcome when they arrived there – including Svetlana Bell, Tom Bell, Andrei and Larissa Elizarkov, and others.

All these people have something to say about the sacred tigers, and a few have seen them!

In Canada, I appreciate my friends, most of them storytellers, some teachers, and a thinker. They have talked thoughtfully and most of them looked over this and other books: Linda Stender, Jane Wintemute, Liz Tanner, Mariella Bertelli, Feloor Talebi, Les Blydo, Ramona Orr, and Philomena Jordon. There have been many pleasurable conversations and improvements to the book.

I especially appreciate Comfort Ero for her fascinating thoughts about similarities between the Udege people and those in some areas of Nigeria, nearly halfway around the world.

Thanks always to Louise Le Blanc – storyteller from the Yukon, and key to my travels and storytelling from the start.

Great thanks to Mark Abley and Richard Ratzlaff for many helpful questions and suggestions and working hard at a difficult time, and others from McGill-Queen's University Press. Thanks also to Kathleen Fraser and Robert MacNevin, and to unknown helpers.

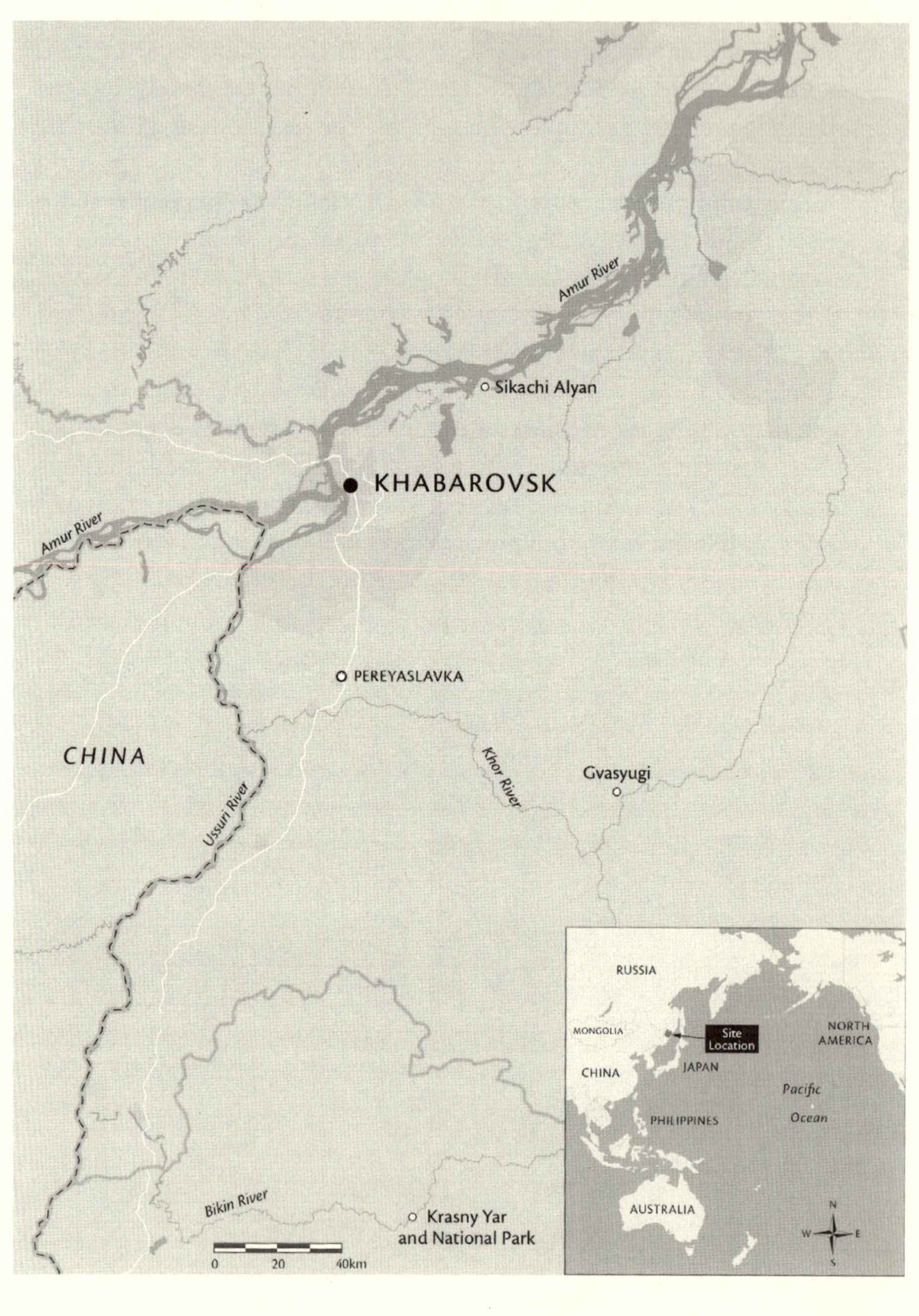
Amur River
Sikachi Alyan
KHABAROVSK
Amur River
PEREYASLAVKA
CHINA
Khor River
Gvasyugi
Ussuri River
Bikin River
Krasny Yar
and National Park
0
20
40km
RUSSIA
MONGOLIA
Site
Location
NORTH
AMERICA
CHINA
JAPAN
Pacific
Ocean
PHILIPPINES
AUSTRALIA
N
W
E
S

NAMES

Most Udege nowadays have Russian first names, as well as their Udege family names with Russian endings. In the past, most had Udege first names as well.

The full form now is: A person's first name – father's name with Russian grammatical ending – family name. For example: Valentina Tunsianovna Kyalundzyuga (note that her father's name, Tunsiana, is an Udege one, whereas her first name is Russian – Valentina). This usage developed when Russian came to their village. In common conversation, the polite form is often Valentina Tunsianovna. In official or written form, it may be Valentina Kyalundzyuga. For people I didn't get to know well, the name in this book is simply the first name and family name. For example: Valentin Hagdaev.

Many people also have a nickname, such as Valya for Valentina or Nadia from Nadezhda. This name stands alone and is used with good friends and relatives. Children also generally use it. Valentina Tunsianovna used Valya when in other countries to make things easier for non-Russian speakers.

Nicknames of affection often have an ending such as Kirochka. For simplicity this doesn't appear in this book.

In stories and legends there are often names that are rarely if ever used by ordinary people. For good characters, we find Belye for a beautiful and intelligent woman. Yegdiga is an excellent male hunter, also highly intelligent. The bad names are Emende, for a woman who is awkward and a bad cook, while Kanda Mafa is often a father who makes trouble for his daughters.

Downtown Khabarovsk with its onion-dome church. Photo by author.

The closest I've come to an elk! This is the zoo outside Khabarovsk. Photo by Alexander Frolenok, used with permission.

The new bridge at Gvasyugi is strong, but has no railings. Villagers take it easily, but we hesitate. Photo by Alexander Frolenok, used with permission.

Boys playing with pots as the ice breaks up in Gvasyugi. Photo by author.

Girl balancing on the ice in Gvasyugi. Photo by author.

Valentina Tunsianovna stands by the statue of Jansi Kimonko, the first published writer in Gvasyugi. Photo by Alexander Frolenok, used with permission.

A fish-skin dress will last a lifetime. This one is made in Troitskoye. Photo by author.

Valentina Tunsianovna puts the bear bone on the tree so that the other bears will know that they are welcome. Photo by author.

Olesia Vladimirovna Shamshur plays bells on a shaman's belt and dances in Gvasyugi. Photo by author.

Embroidering helps to keep evil spirits away from openings in clothing.
This collar was made by Valentina Tunsianovna. Photo by author.

The story of a hungry tiger and a clever girl, illustrated by the popular Khabarovsk artist Gennadi Pavlishin. Photo by author.

Valentina Tunsianovna speaks with spirits on the mountain top between Gvasyugi and Krasny Yar. Photo by Alexander Frolenok, used with permission.

A demonstration of how to soften animal skin, given at the new museum in Krasny Yar. Photo by author.

Polina Ilinichna Sun is a singer and has two sisters. One is a hunter and the other is a teacher. Polina lives in Krasny Yar. Photo by author.

Alexander Kanchuga is a linguist, teacher, and an expert on shamanism. He lives in Krasny Yar. Photo by author.

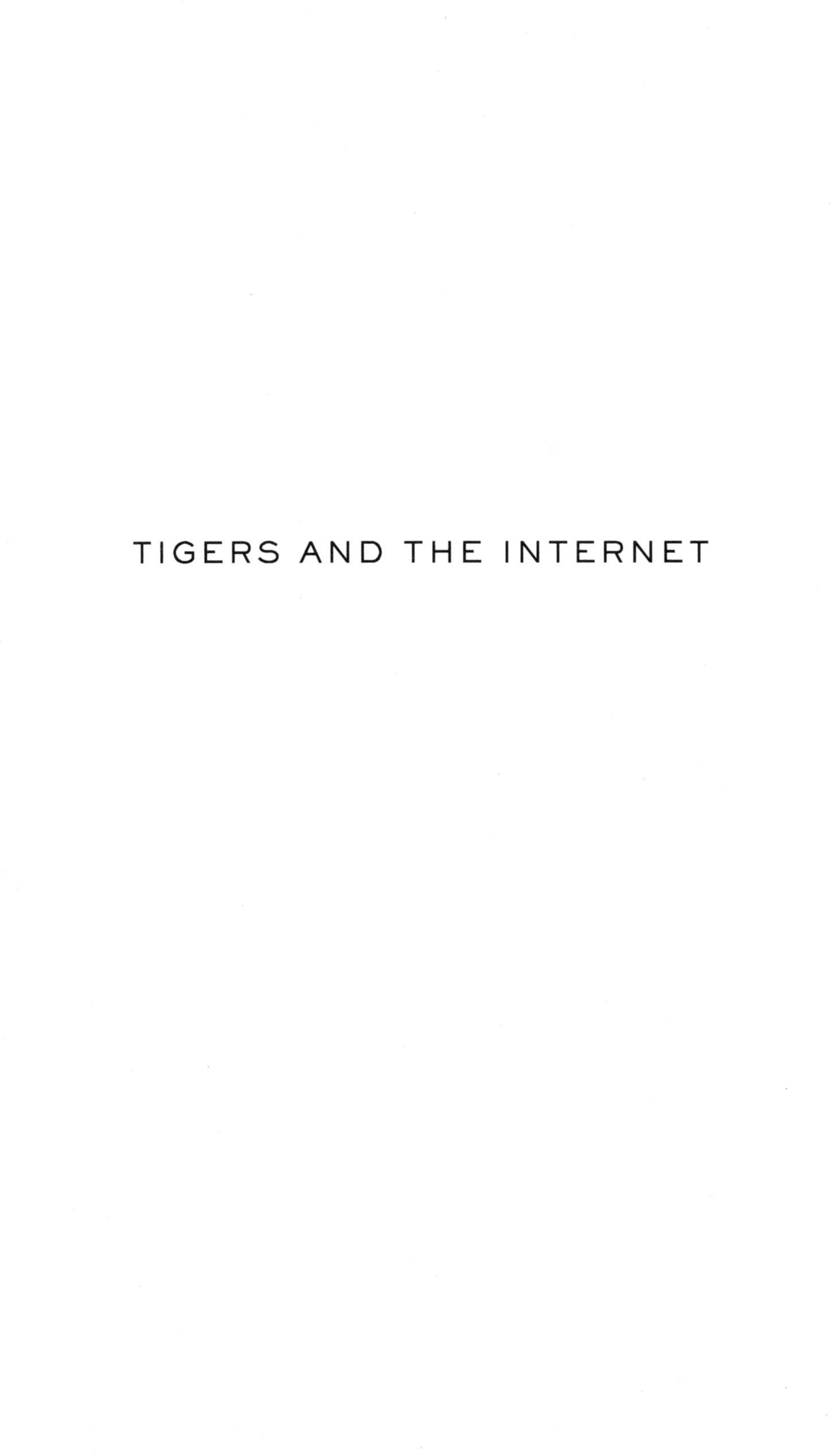

TIGERS AND THE INTERNET

INTRODUCTION

The Udege people live in the Russian Far East, between the border of Manchuria and the sea. The world's largest tigers live right there, and tigers are sacred to the people. From time beyond memory, the two have agreed not to harm each other. People say that this agreement has been kept truly, unless the tiger is ill. Just one of the local men claimed he had seen a tiger in those olden days, and he was known to exaggerate. Most people had never seen even one of them in the wild.

Twenty years ago, the forests were larger than they are now, which made more space for the tigers to stay away from people. Now they are seen more frequently. Little by little the logging has come closer to their habitat, and tigers are known to be seen even in the villages of Gvasyugi and Krasny Yar, where the Udege live. One day in 2005, a young village woman saw a tiger right outside her kitchen window. She was first shocked and then worried he would step on her delicious tomatoes while looking for meat. Later, her mother showed me the animal's scratches on a tree beside the river that we had just walked across.

The people of these villages live the spiritual and practical lives of their ancestors – hunting and gathering. Skilled shamans help to heal the ills of people and animals, predict the weather, and help the dead go to the other world. Meanwhile things change. Many of the same people have university degrees and teach in the schools, while others are doctors in hospitals and clinics.

When I arrived in April of 2019, it was far from the first time. I had come back from my home in western Canada to see friends who live in two villages and the city of Khabarovsk. Nadezhda Kimonko lives in the large city, and Valentina Kyalundzyuga in the small village of Gvasyugi. We had known each other for twenty years, and it was time to see them again after a long gap.

After an easy day in the city to get used to the time zones, Nadezhda and I set off to see Valentina Tunsianovna and other old friends.

Alex Frolenok was an excellent driver for the four-hour trip to the village and beyond. We started close to the Amur River in the centre of the city, where two tall churches stand. They had certainly not been there in Soviet times, when religion was not allowed. When that time was fully over, around 1990, the churches were built specifically beside the river, so that the Chinese could see the power of Russia with its golden onion domes on high. The Chinese are only thirty kilometres away, and the Russians were afraid the Chinese would move into their territory, since Siberia has so much more space. The churches were to stop them. But that was nearly twenty years ago, with religion allowed and China concerned with other things.

Nearby there are decorative buildings with red and green walls, along with trim in white and black. They may go back over several centuries and now the stores contain everything from clothing to food, and even banks. Further up, tanks and soldiers used to pass through an empty square on holidays. This meant there was no space for a fountain, but now it has one, and elegant benches to rest on, with trees above.

As we set off in Alex's car, the wide Amur River was behind us. Buses and cars hurried past well-dressed people who never seem to smile – at least at foreigners they don't know. As far as clothes go, people in Khabarovsk have always been willing to use as much of their money as needed – to be classy. The clothes are often European if they can afford it. And, of course, there are workers with old worn clothes on the streets as well. Most of the faces are Russian, while occasionally you may see Koreans or Japanese, who also have lived in the city for generations. A few Udege may appear as well, either visiting or working, but you might take them for Japanese, since some Udege look similar to them.

As we got farther from the oldest parts of the city, we came to the bookstore where I buy my maps. The old one had been left at home, ragged, so we stopped for a few minutes. Next, we passed a large park and later old apartment buildings that all look alike; they were from the Soviet period, and the rooms are very small. Behind them are large pipes that carry hot water long distances overground to all the buildings – hot at the beginning and chilly at the end.

After a while, the road took us out of the city, through towns and then farms. We turned off after an hour or so and stopped at the only gas station. Soon we were on a rough dirt road with no more buildings. Up the mountain, which was mostly covered with ash trees and a few of the stunning white birches whose leaves were just coming out at the end of April.

At last, Nadezhda pointed to the right. "This is it!" The road got even narrower and darker with trees, but soon a dog ran out barking and then houses appeared. We stopped at last. It felt as though we had bounced and bumped for a lot longer than four hours. We stretched our legs and looked at the river just behind the houses. I felt at home.

The first time I arrived there, in 1993, was in summer. A woman was driving a motorcycle with a sidecar. I'll always remember how she told us what it was like before she had it. She had seen a tiger on the way along the eight kilometres from another village – every day she walked from home to work. She had run, but luckily the tiger had not followed her.

Rhododendrons, forsythia, lilies, and daisies were blooming everywhere that year. Gardens with tomatoes, cucumbers, and corn too. This time it was too early for that. Men were fishing and already preparing firewood for the next year's winter. The people in this small, isolated village had few material things, but gave us a warm welcome as always. Nadezhda showed the way to one of the houses.

The Udege people number only about two thousand altogether, even though the census is rarely taken. The people include those in the two small villages, and the rest are spread through Khabarovsk and beyond. Their land is well known abroad for its ginseng and the revered Siberian tiger, although it also has magnificent rivers and mountains.

In this book we will look at Udege arts, dance, music, and storytelling traditions, in addition to enjoying the plentiful energy and good humour of the people. Community activities, history, and politics are active, as is spirituality, including shamanism and other simpler forms of healing, such as predicting the future. It's hard to remember that our friendship began shortly after the Soviet period ended.

In April 2019, I found that things had changed radically in the years since I was last there. Now, for the first time, many villagers have cellphones, even if the Internet rarely comes there, while city people have reached out globally. There is running water and a washing machine in at least one of Gvasyugi's houses, while in the past everyone took water in buckets from the river. Most still do.

Even when I was last there in 2005, they had only limited electricity, no phones or running water, and only a few cars – most of them ready to break down at the drop of a hat. The weather station had very little equipment then, but the only way to send information to the city was by using what they had; it was sometimes used also for medical emergencies. Teachers and labourers worked hard.

There was a bakery with delicious bread, but no other store. The people of the area loved their home, and still do – with its fast-rolling rivers and distant tall mountains, wooden boats, profuse flowers, and a fascinating history.

In 2019, there was a sad event. Valentina Tunsianovna's house burned to the ground, taking her books, clothing, bedding, and her daughters' belongings. It was fortunate no one was hurt and that most of her books had been published. Now she shares a small room with another woman.[1]

Money is still a problem for the elderly, although when I was first here they had practically no money at all. Food came from their relatives' hunting and their own gardens. Now they have a little from the grocery as well.

The financial difference among villagers is probably more significant now. It is not easy for Indigenous people, still plagued with racism and loss of land – as with Indigenous people in Canada and many other places. These things change very slowly.

Another Udege village is Krasny Yar, to the south of Gvasyugi. Just that far away, they find themselves in a different climate. They may have similar trees as their northern neighbours, such as larch, cedar, and oak, but they also have southern plants, such as grapes, lotus, ginseng plants, and opium poppies. Ferns may grow five feet tall in Krasny Yar.

Tigers live in both places, although they are rarely seen. Bears and smaller animals do come out more often, and the hunters find them.

The people have different issues since their land was chosen a few years ago for a national park. This has made for tourism, largely Russian, as well as some disagreement. Some of the locals had been for the park, while others were concerned that they would no longer be able to hunt, which gives them their main source of meat. Too much space would be given to the tourists to allow hunting. As it has worked out, most enjoy the benefits – things like a new medical clinic. Others yearn for the past, when the land was all theirs.[2]

In both places, people are occupied with the values that they most want to preserve. There are many important Indigenous keepers of culture among the Udege, with a strong dedication to the people of their homeland.

My friends have a great desire to have their work, and even their existence, known in the outside world, which is part of why I write and speak about them. Many Canadians have heard me tell Udege stories over the years, and some heard Valentina Kyalundzyuga and Nadezhda Kimonko themselves at festivals in Vancouver and Whitehorse in 1998.

For many years, Valentina Tunsianovna has gathered and published ancient tales in two languages. Russian is one of them, and and the other is one of the twelve living languages in the Tungus family, of which Udege is one.

Nadezhda Kimonko teaches dancers and storytellers. Then there are the magnificent illustrations of Gennadi Pavlishin, with elegant borders and recognizable men and women that everyone in the villages knows.

Pavel Sulyandziga is one of the Udege leaders, and speaks for his people at the United Nations and beyond. For years, Yevdokia Batovna helped people with her healings and stories. Vasili Dunkai is a working shaman, as are three others: Victoria Donkan, Vera Onenko, and Elena Kilye. Lyubov Passar is occupied with a number of global organizations and works as a medical doctor. Oksana Zvidennaya works intelligently with politics and culture, while Alexander Kanchuga is a teacher of everything from language to history and shamanism.

In the earlier years, my purpose was anthropological research in storytelling and its connection with shamanism, which I had found in Inuit, Tuvan, and Khakassian cultures. I'm also a performing storyteller and musician. At first people in Russia could not understand the odd connection between these jobs. Finally, they gave it up and decided, "She's a good person," which I find an honourable title. This time I wanted to see how things had changed in various ways, including local politics. Connections had been made by email, which of course was not possible in those early days, and now we use Internet.

I had been fortunate to visit during a short opening of about three to ten years following the fall of the Soviet Union. Elders were still alive who remembered the old stories and were pleased to tell them to a foreigner, especially one who could speak Russian. Some of the stories felt very strange to me and to my listeners back home. But people in the villages were willing and able to explain – as much as a story can be explained.

By 2019, at least twenty of those elders were gone, and many of the others had forgotten the stories in favour of television. Now a new era is emerging, with beautiful new books and teachers who use them in their classrooms and with the public. Udege speakers and sometimes neighbouring peoples have classes, including storytelling, that are connected to the active dancers.

Because Indigenous languages and stories that included religion of any sort were forbidden under communism, cultural workers spent less time on storytelling than on the more acceptable arts of dance, song, sewing, embroidery, and woodwork. At one time, drinking alcohol was also forbidden, which was very difficult for Russians, but less so for the Udege, many of whom do not drink. Soviet-era storytelling no longer conveyed the important aspects of Indigenous history – their sense of humour, intricate artwork, poetic intonation, and political expression. Most important of all is their spirituality, based on the land, water, animals, and people.

Indigenous children have read Russian stories in school instead of hearing their own, and for the most part grown-ups have begun to read or to watch TV instead of listening to stories being told. Many things had been improved but these vital parts of culture were nearly lost. Now they work hard to bring those ancient understandings back in a new era.

Storytelling lived in kitchens and by campfires. Now it continues in festivals and bilingual storytelling contests, books, and language learning, although dance is still the favourite for the youth. Arts, including embroidery and woodwork, are enjoyed and also sold to tourists, not only Russians but occasional Europeans, Koreans, and Japanese.

Tigers and the Internet has seven chapters. Each is centred on one or more of the people I have mentioned, along with their work and interests. Each has a story gathered by Valentina Kyalundzyuga around 1960. That was when she realized that as a people they were in danger of losing this great treasure and was first to put the ancient tales down on paper.

Although now there are many options, including the Internet, for a long time, history was recorded primarily in books. Even longer ago it was passed on only orally. This was the case in Gvasyugi. The stories have been told by many people, male and female. Valentina gathered elders to sit together, listening and telling tales, and to enjoy passing them to each other. Later, she had a book published, reproducing all the stories with permission. In this book, the storyteller's name appears with each title.

An oral story could be repeated and be quite different every time. Many storytellers like to say that they have passed them exactly as they heard them, but inevitably there are subtle changes. This may even be affected by the listeners – their moods or the weather.

It seems to me that the oral story often has more detail and variety than the written form, especially if the history concerns ordinary people, rather than heroes. We can't say how ancient these tales are, but it is quite possible many have been told for two thousand years, with changes here and there. History has also been part of the oral tradition for a very long time.

The Udege have three forms of stories. One, called *nimanku*, comes largely from dreams. The second, *telungu*, comes from things that really happened, no matter how magical they seem to us. And the last is *exe*, stories in song. When you listen to or read a story, don't expect it to be realistic. You may be hearing something that seems impossible, but it will often have an important underlying message.

To start the book, there is a legend, likely a *telungu*. It comes from the name of a river, and is about a crocodile. The story was told by the elder Yengili Batovich Kimonko, one of the storytellers who often met together on evenings, telling stories in the Udege language. Many did not read. Valentina Kyalundzyuga started the evenings around 1960, and they continued until 1998. Amost all of the stories here have come from Valentina's book, *Памятники Фольклора Народов Сибири и Дальнего Востока. Фольклор, Удэгейцев, Ниманку, Тэлунгу, Ехэ* (*Monuments of Folklore of the Peoples of Siberia and the Far East: Folklore, Udege, Telengu, Ekhe*). The translations are mine.

Clearly the animals in these stories do not live anywhere near the Udege now, but the oral history of elders say that the climate was once warmer than it is currently, and that the animals themselves have changed. On the other hand, in chapter 2 we will see two versions of the story "Two Suns," as told by Indigenous people in Taiwan and the Russian Far East. This could indicate that the story has migrated, though we don't know when and how.

Reddish Water

An ancient legend says that, at some time long ago, on a river with red water, there lived a terrible crocodile. Hunters were afraid to go near. But one time they decided to get revenge on the crocodile. They filled birchbark containers with good food. Coming closer to the crocodile, the hunters began to throw the containers at him. Swallowing them, the crocodile grew pot-bellied and fat. Then the hunters decided to fool the animal, and they ran between two birch trees. The watching crocodile crawled after them and got caught between the trees. He couldn't move either backward or forward, and so he choked there. From that time people started to call this river "Khulalgi," which means "red water."

The connection of crocodiles and red water is common in the many tales of the animals, even if that connection is not entirely clear. It may have to do with the crocodile's red blood. On the other hand, Valentina Tunsianovna said there is a swamp far away up the Khor River, where the water is red from mineral deposits. People say there used to be crocodiles in that swamp, who chased people and ate them.

Nadezhda remembers that her grandmother used to tell stories about monkeys and crocodiles, which she didn't believe. Others say that crocodiles, elephants, and monkeys had names in their own languages, which made it seem they had been there for many years in the past. Later we will see a number of stories about the *singmu*, which means crocodile in the Udege language. As mentioned, oral history also shows that either the area was warmer at one time or that the people had moved from even further south. We'll see in other stories that crocodiles were burned with birchbark and thrown in the water. The crocodiles took the flaming birchbark in their mouths and died.

1

YEVDOKIA BATOVNA KYALUNDZYUGA
History, Story, and Shamanism Long Ago

Yevdokia Batovna's last words to me came as we sat together waiting for my ride back to the city. From there I would fly home to Canada. I asked to take her picture. As soon as the camera clicked, she said, "This is the last time we will see each other in this life."

I found no words to reply to such certainty. The next year I returned, and she was still alive, although away seeing relatives. The time after that, she was gone.

I met Yevdokia Batovna around 1995 in the village of Gvasyugi. She was already elderly at that time and died in 1998. My favourite village in Russia is there – rivers crossed with homemade bridges, horses munching across from the school, and children playing. She lived in the middle of it. She was an honoured elder and a relative of my friends Valentina Tunsianovna and Nadezhda Efimovna. She was also the sister of Jansi Kimonko, and a statue of him stands on the grass in the village. He was the first published writer among the Udege people.

A year before, I'd heard of Auntie Dusia, as I learned to call her, who was an excellent storyteller and a reader of energy. But she had refused to see me, a foreigner. The next year, Nadezhda convinced her. She invited us in, giving us both energy readings, using light forked sticks that she brought out of a box. We all sat in the kitchen on low chairs near each other, the way Udege people did in those days. Nadia and I held our sticks toward each other loosely at the end as Auntie Dusia watched. Our two sticks connected in the middle after the ends had been dipped in water. They moved up and down, together and apart, in answer to our personal questions. Auntie Dusia interpreted the movements and spoke – her replies were kept only for us. Mine told something about how my life would go in the future. Nadia's was her own. I'm pleased to say both of us have been successful. I had learned of this at home in North America, where it was called Dowsing.

Yevdokia Batovna was quite a character, and definitely partook of ancient ways. An expert with plant medicine, she made her own thread out of elk sinew and used it for sewing hide clothing. She stuck a knife into the threshold at night to protect her home – unfortunately all villagers have to lock up one way or another. Several of her songs have been field recorded, and some of her fascinating stories go back into the history of her people, including those with tigers and bears.

As well as showing how to see the future, she told me stories – a woman with a great sense of humour. It was sometimes hard to understand her Russian, partly because some of her teeth were missing, and partly because it was a second language for both of us. I'm not sure if she could read and write, but she certainly had a great memory. Nonetheless, I listened to my recordings over at home and could make sense of the stories she told. Unfortunately, my field recordings have become inacessible.

The stories and transcriptions Auntie Dusia recounted were also translated from the original Udege language into Russian by Valentina Kyalundzyuga, and my memories now partake of both.

There's a lot to think about in this first long story, probably one of the most ancient tales. It is one of a number that begin with the first people. It shows how they got started in their relationships with animals, especially bears and tigers, which were to become sacred. Finally, the people turned into the Udege. The story has been told by many ancestors.

Was it acceptable at some time for brother and sister to marry in a deep forest with no one else there? Apparently it was – at an earlier time among those who were to survive. Moving often, they may not have met many people who were not related to them. In fact, it was likely they did not meet any others at all. It's also likely that they married for practical reasons as well as love, since people needed partners in order to survive. Even now there are people who live in the forests, and are not known to the government.

In some of our stories, "marriage" does not always come with a ceremony, as other marriages in our stories do. It's more like an agreement among the two. Even now in some countries people marry relatives, though this is not accepted in others.

Clearly this was a transition period. In this story, marriage of sister and brother had become unacceptable to them at some more recent point in time, but it continued through deceit. The story has many problems for not only those two, but also their children, sadly for all. And yet, in the end, they became the Udege people. It also shows relationships not only among men and women, but with animals as well. (The elk will come later.) Many things are also explained about eating bear meat and how the traditional house was built. Other things cannot be explained, such as a human woman who turns into an elk and then dies in both forms. Storytellers rarely explain difficult answers.

Auntie Dusia told stories with great expression and humour. Although many people like to tell stories at night, she told this one in the afternoon. Her style had a coy humour and made me laugh frequently.

Sister and Brother

A brother and sister lived together. They grew up and started to live. One day the sister said, "Let's go find people to live with. A wife for you and a man for me. How can we go on living like this?"

There was no one living near them.

He said, "How will I find someone? Upstream or down."

It seems this must have been in winter. The brother thought, "How will I find someone? My sister says I have to. I don't know anyone. There's no one nearby. All right, I'll go in the early morning." He said to his sister, "Make my breakfast early."

"Why?"

"I'm going. If you won't find a wife for me, I will do it for myself. I'll have to go and look for a wife."

She had been dreaming for a long time about marrying her brother. She got up early and boiled food.

They went outside.

"Where will I go?" asked the brother. "There's no one nearby. Where to go? Upstream or down? All right, I'll go down."

As soon as he was gone, she went back inside and got ready to go herself. And she too went downstream. After her brother? Nobody knows. She didn't go by the river but flew somehow, in the air. She got ahead of him. Probably she flew. They travelled and travelled. She was up in the air and he down on the ground.

Then it was time to stop for the night, and they both stopped. He said to himself, "We had everything at home. Firewood, everything. I should go back there." Not above but below. He thought, "Where will I spend the night? There's nothing here."

Then he noticed smoke and a hut. People must be there. He went closer and looked. It was exactly like their place: a barn, firewood, and a house. "Whoever lives here is just like us," he thought.

He approached. There were no dogs. A woman came out. He thought, "She looks exactly like my sister." And indeed, his sister had got there first.

She said, "Where did you come from? Nobody ever comes here, not even a crow. Not even a bird. Nobody at all."

"My sister said I should go looking for a wife. That's why I left home."

She got cooking! They ate. And all that time it was his sister. She disguised herself, or fooled him.

"I don't care where I go," he said. "I just need to find a wife."

"But I want to get married too! There are no people here," she said. They ate. And then sat and talked, but he was embarrassed, because she was just like his sister.

"It's hard for me living alone," she said. So, in a moment he agreed to stay with her, and they lay down to sleep.

After some time, he said, "I need to go see my sister." He wanted to see how she was doing. Maybe she needed firewood, he thought, but somehow he didn't want to go. Maybe he felt in his soul that something was wrong.

And she said, "Why don't you go see your sister? Go tomorrow. Maybe she's hungry. Maybe she died."

So he went.

As soon as he was gone, she got things together and flew back to where they had lived before. She took everything – the barns, the firewood, the house.

He got there and then stopped, thinking, "My sister is probably not alive." But then he saw smoke. "Thank God she is alive."

He came to the house, and she came out. "Oh brother, here you are alive. I thought you were dead."

She cooked dinner. They ate.

"How are you?" she asked. And in fact she had married her brother!

"Oh, I don't know. I met somebody just like you. Her dress, the house, all exactly like ours."

"Oh, there are all kinds of people," she sighed.

He didn't want to go back to his wife. Instead, he went hunting, thinking, "What is all this about?"

"Why don't you go back to your wife?" asked his sister after a while.

"There's something wrong. She's just like you in every way, even her dress."

"Oh, there are all kinds of people." Again, she says, "Why don't you go back? After all, you're married."

"Yes, something's wrong. She's just like you."

She wanted to be married to him again, and urged him to go.

"All right," he said. "I'll go tomorrow."

As soon as he was gone, she flew away in an instant. She took everything, barns, house, firewood.

"Who knows if my wife is still alive?" he thought. Then he saw the smoke. "Thank God she's alive."

"Was your sister alive?" his wife asked.

"Yes, she's fine." Still that feeling that something's wrong.

So they started to eat.

"How's your sister?"

"Fine."

Time went by and she gave birth to a boy and a girl. I don't remember which was first. Then he went hunting every day, killing all the animals until there was nothing left nearby. So he had to go further, to the place where he had lived before. And there he killed an elk.

Why he was like that and got fooled, I don't know.

He killed the elk and started dragging it home whole. When he got near home, he left it there, on purpose. He didn't take the skin off. He didn't know, but he probably felt something. He left his arrow there in the elk.

"If I'm really living with my sister," he said to himself, "I will have killed her. I'll leave my arrow here. If I'm really living with my sister, there will be a mark on her chest."

"Where have you been for so long?" his wife asked when he returned. "We were hungry, waiting for you."

"I was far away and killed an elk. I brought it home whole and left it nearby. Tomorrow, son, you go and get the animal."

The boy agreed. The next day he went out and a bird spoke to him.

He came back and said, "Mama, make me an arrow. I want to kill a bird."

"Don't go far," she replied, and made the arrow without question.

He went and shot at the bird that started to talk to him in the Udege language. "What a bad family," said the bird. "A brother is living with his sister, and now the boy is doing this to me."

The boy ran home.

"Mama I went along the river and shot a bird who talked." He told her what the bird had said.

"When your father comes home, don't tell him."

His father came home late. The boy didn't say anything, and they started to eat.

"Papa, today I went down the river –"

"Don't bother your father," his mother interrupted.

She must have guessed what the boy would say. They finished eating. She was very tired and lay down. She lay down early.

Then Papa said to his son, "What did you want to say before, when we were eating?"

"Oh Papa, I went along the river and shot a bird and almost killed it. But I just hit the fluff. She talked to me and said, "That woman is living with her brother."

Next morning the woman cooked, and then took the sled and, instead of the boy, she went off into the *taiga*, the forest on the mountains.

The father told her, "You'll go a long way. There's no animal to take you there."

"Never mind, there will be tracks."

They waited and waited, but she didn't come back. He guessed she was the animal he had shot.

They ate, and then he couldn't sleep and went outdoors. But she had taken the sled.

He walked and walked, and then he saw her there, dead. He took out the arrow and took the elk. He left his wife. He got home, and it was dark. The children were crying – there was no fire and no light. He didn't go inside, but made a fire outside. He lived there for several days and didn't feed his children and didn't eat himself. To live with your own sister is a sin. He was a long time there outside, without going into the hut. Finally, he loaded up the sleigh, made a cut in the ankle of each child, put a strap through, and hitched them to the sleigh. He tied them to the sleigh – the girl too, she was also there. And off he went.

He drove them day and night, without a break, without food. He drove further, and finally the boy tore off at the place where he was attached. He fell down and died. But the girl stayed there with her father. She pulled and pulled and pulled the sleigh, and also got torn off at the ankle.

He didn't realize it and left her behind.

She cried there. "Where's Papa?"

Then a brown bear came along.

"Why are you crying?"

She told him what her papa had done.

"Don't cry, I'll take you home." She got up on his back.

"Hold on tight." It was dark.

"There is my house," said the bear. It was that thing that bears make, a lair. He took her to his den but then stopped outside. "I won't take you in there. You'll sleep here. I'll dig in there and you stay here. Tomorrow I'll make you a house."

He got up in the morning and started bringing in wood. He made the house well. All good on the outside, with a nice bed inside. "Don't be afraid of me," he said. "I won't do anything bad to you."

They lived there and she grew up.

Then he said to her, "Now I'm going to find you a husband. I'll find you the very best! Just don't worry and don't go away. Every day I'll go looking.

He looked and looked. Once he saw the tracks of a *Mergen*, a fine hunter – the man's tracks went one way, and the bear's crossed them. He went home to his den. He went through the hole in the wall, to his own place.

He explained this. "First people will come – hunters. You tell them you're alone, that there's no one here. If they ask about my den, tell them it just happens to be like that."

And he went away. Toward evening, one young hunter came. Looking at the hole in the wall, the hunter said, "What is this?"

"Ahh, it's just like that. When I first started to live here it was just like that."

"She fooled him," said Auntie Dusia.

They got ready to spend the night. She cooked, they ate. He asked again, "What is that outside," and again she didn't tell him.

"It was like that when I was small," she said.

"How do you live, alone?"

"As I remember, when I was small, I started to live alone. My father and mother died." She fooled him.

They ate. He asked, "Are you alone? I'm alone too. I have no one. I live alone in the woods. Let's get married."

She had already grown up and said, "All right, let's."

"You're alone and I'm alone. I have no parents." And so he stayed.

Next day he went hunting. The bear came home and said to her, "Today I will test him to see if he is strong. Don't be afraid. Don't tell him I am a bear. I'll cry out, and he will jump out to see what is happening and he'll freeze."

The bear went out. "If he kills me, don't you eat my meat. These two places only you can eat, and nothing else." He showed her the places on his buttocks and then went away.

Again, the man came. They lay down to sleep and talked. Then from outside that brown bear cried out. The fellow didn't put anything on but ran out in his bare feet. She was afraid and waited till morning to go out. The man was scared and had frozen to death. "Oh, poor thing," she said, looking at him.

Then the bear came again in the evening.

"Why did you do that? To kill a person," she said.

"I told you I would find a very strong man. Brave, and not afraid of anything. Again, I will come and bring a hunter. Don't tell him anything, and don't be afraid. I want you to find a very kind person so that you will live well."

The bear went away.

In the evening a fellow came. You could see from his tracks that he was stronger than the first one.

"Let's spend the night," he said.

They ate, and he asked, "Are you alone?"

"I'm alone."

"What's that hole there?"

"Oh, I remember when I was little it was already there." She was fooling him. Again, she agreed to get married, and they laid down. They talked.

Again, the bear cried out, and the man ran out barefoot to kill the bear, but he didn't succeed. It was dark, scary, how could she go out? She also didn't hear the bear's voice. She sat and sat there that night and when it got light, she went out. The man had frozen there beside the threshold. He wanted to shoot but hadn't succeeded.

Again, she asked the bear and he said, "I told you long ago that I would find someone strong." He went into the *taiga* along the mountains.[1]

Toward evening he came, that brown one.

"Girl, again I found tracks and this one must be even stronger." He came and said, "I found this man …" That's what he said.

And then he went away, without eating. Again, a man came. He was good-looking! Strong, young.

"Are you alone?" he asked.

"Yes, I've always been alone. I remember when I was little I was already alone."

"How do you get your food and firewood?"

"They come to me themselves."

This man asked, "Who do you live with?"

"With no one."

"What is that hole?"

"I remember when I was little it was like that. I don't know."

"When you were little, who brought you up?"

"I don't know."

"Well, if you don't have anyone, let's get married."

Again, they laid down to sleep.

"This was the third time already!" said Auntie Dusia with a sly grin.

They started to tell each other about how they had lived. Then suddenly that bear cried out. That hunter, *Mergen*, didn't run right out but quickly got dressed and then went out.[2]

He came back and said, "Girl, I don't know if you will want to kill me. I don't know if it was your father or your brother, but I killed him."

She told him that the bear had said someone would come and kill him.

"Who was he to you?"

"She didn't tell," said Auntie Dusia with a coy grin.

A man had lived with his sister and given birth to a boy and a girl.

In the morning, she went out. Right there on the threshold, he had killed the bear. He was such a strong man.

"As you like, if you want to kill me," he said.

"I am a woman, how can I kill you? He ordered it himself. He told me to use the bones to make a house, to take the skin and everything. The skin will cover the house. He told me to take the meat from those two places but nowhere else. You of course can eat the rest."

"Who was he? Your father?"

She didn't tell.

They started to live well. It turned into the kind of house our people used to live in, using bones. They lived and she gave birth to a boy and a girl as her mother had. They both lived, the two of them. And the smaller child said, "I will tell you part of the way we lived – the most awful thing. Papa killed mama."

Why, I don't know. Her brother killed her. Maybe he was a bear, not a person. I don't know. They lived together a long time and she gave birth to a boy and a girl."

Once later a man came to their place, thin, torn, all ragged and in bad shape. He was her father. How would she know this was her father? She wanted to bring him home. It's cold to live outside, to sleep and prepare firewood.

But he didn't stay. "I'll turn into a deer," he said, and went to live in the *taiga*." ▾

Vladimir Arsenyev's Notes on Yevdokia Batovna's Story[3]

Vladimir Arsenyev (1872–1930) gathered many stories from the Udege and other peoples of the Russian Far East during the late-nineteenth and early-twentieth centuries. He came to the area as an explorer, and wrote many books about it. The most famous was *Dersu Uzala*, about his military work with the help of a native hunter of that name. This is largely remembered in the excellent Japanese film by Akira Kurosawa.

At the time, the area was filled with trouble between Russians, Chinese, and the Udege. His military work may have caused the death of many Indigenous people owing to his finding them and telling others how they could be found.

Whether or not Yevdokia Batovna was aware of his books, Arsenyev heard a number of versions of the story "Sister and Brother," and they can be found in his Russian translations. I'll mention here a few striking differences between them and Yevdokia Batovna's.

In at least one version of the story, the girl *marries* the bear, and from them come the Oroch people – a group similar to the Udege. Her brother, who has not died in this version, is a good hunter and accidentally kills the bear.

After the death of the mother, the father takes the girl to a bear and the brother to a female tiger, and then he kills himself. All Udege people came from that marriage with the bear, while no children came from the tiger. The bear is an ancestor, and both animals are totems.

The tiger helped the boy and explained to him that, from then on, they would not harm each other. "Now you are big, you can live yourself. I have fed you, and so in the future you will never touch a tiger. I too will not do evil to people."

In one version, the men who tried to marry the girl came from a very dangerous group – the Nengui – the most frightful of Udege folklore.

The best man who eventually married the girl is Yegda, who was ordered to do so by the highest deity, *Enduri*.

Yevdokia Batovna's Life in the 1990s and the Family in 2019

What of her daily life outside the spiritual? I wondered where she had lived in childhood – something I had never asked before. I'd always thought of her largely as a storyteller. When I visited again, Auntie Dusia was no longer with us, but not forgotten. I asked Valentina Tunsianovna in 2019 what family she had had and what work she had done. Was she born in Gvasyugi or elsewhere? Valentina said she wouldn't tell me, since Yevdokia Batovna's three daughters would know best. Two of them live in Gvasyugi now, and the third in Krasny Yar, and we would be going there soon. Through the three of them I saw her described by her family. Valentina

Tunsianovna herself told me of her son. After saying this, she wouldn't tell me anything more!

The two daughters who lived in Gvasyugi agreed to visit, and immediately asked why they hadn't met me before. We laughed, since I had wondered the same thing. We made ourselves comfortable on bright-coloured cushions in the house we were staying in, thanks to the generosity of the owners. The two daughters in Gvasyugi are Larissa Ilinichna Kyalundzyuga and Nelli Ilinichna Andreeva (born Kyalundzyuga). The women went on to answer questions.

Yevdokia Batovna's name in Udege was Yegodya. This was probably Russified into Yevdokia. Her own parents had many children, since her father had two wives, one of them her mother. Yevdokia Batovna also had a sister and a cousin.

She had seven children. Four boys died, and three girls survived. One of them, Larissa, went away from home for schooling in an *internat*, or residential school. She became a teacher and still works at the Gvasyugi school. Nelli, the second daughter, went hunting with her mother without schooling.

"We two lived in a tent," Nelli says. "The shape is similar to a small house, with a way to open the top while putting on skis or clothes. It was handy for standing up fully."

Her sister added that the tent has a shape similar to those used by tourists, but with a *kamin*, a fireplace, in the middle and smoke holes on the sides. The women were emphatic that the tent is not a yurt, which is used more on the flats, where there are few trees.

They laughed and asked, "How could we live like that in winter?" Larissa says she was frightened of the hunt when they were younger. But she appreciates that a hunter always brought meat and fish home.

"Our mother had a talent for healing, and she helped many people by using natural remedies. She was shy with people she didn't know well, since she didn't have medical training, although she was very effective," said Nelli.

"In spite of her modesty, she knew a lot," said Larissa. The two speak of *dudnik* as a medicine their mother had invented herself for cancer. They were unsure about the ingredients, which I imagine were all out of the forest or the garden.[4]

"She helped hunters frequently, and as a result no one would steal from her," said one.

I wasn't sure if the hunters tended to steal otherwise, and if they watched out for her. Probably the latter. The hunters would go out looking for whatever animals, birds, or fish they could find. To get an elk or a black bear would be a great haul, and they would share it with others. To steal or withhold from one's own catch is nearly unthinkable.

"Our mother only closed the door when Gypsies, Moldavians, and others came around," said the other.

I was surprised that either Romany or Moldovians had ever found themselves in such a faraway place as Gvasyugi, but they insisted it was so, and I took their word for it. Later I learned that, during the Stalinist period, many Romany from central Russia and Moldovians from Moldova were deported to the Russian Far East, Siberia, and Central Asia.

"During the Second World War, men were away in the army," said Nelli. "Women helped their neighbours to survive with their children. All sorts of strangers might have come through."

In fact, Yevdokia Batovna lived most of her life with war and Soviet power. Very few people of that age live in the village now.

"There were many children around," said Larissa. "And our mother made beautiful designs on all the children's clothing. She looked after them – her own and those of others – and worked with designs in skins."

"She also taught, as Larissa does now," said Nelli. "At first there was no interest in the Udege language," she said, but now there is. Valentina Tunsianovna has made books in several levels for the school.

"Mother kept a good garden, with vegetables and flowers, so as to keep the children and others supplied with food and pleasure."

The women recall the cherries with special happiness. At other times there would be corn and potatoes, I'm sure.

"During wartime, mother worked as a hunter in a *kolkhoz*, a collective farm. She always shared her hunt, and also worked with horses."

I asked the two about the knife Yevdokia Batovna set up in the door at night. They pooh-poohed that, saying that everyone did it. An extra doubling of the locks.

Polina Ilinichna Sun is the third daughter, and she lives in Krasny Yar. We visited in the short time we had in the village, and her husband sat with her, clearly proud of her beauty and talent. His last name is a Chinese one – Sun – and he has lived in Krasny Yar for many years. We sat together with Alex

Frolenok and Nadezhda Kimonko as the rain poured outside. We explained that we had visited with her sisters to find out more about their mother.

They prepared tea.

Polina's sisters say she knows more than they, but once we got there, she denied it, "Of course they know all that I do." She then added to the others' memories that their mother Yevdokia Batovna had made special ceremonies on holidays with music and dance. During the war, she carried a very heavy load, and worked a lot with children who played in their barn.

"Our mother's husband went to the Second World War, while she stayed at home and sewed for soldiers as well as for the children. In that time, her husband was one of the soldiers who managed to come back alive.

"Everyone had to be careful with firewood in the *kamin* fireplace," Polina recalls. "Beside that, they did not have a cow. She made prayer totems for people in many of the houses, not from Buddhist or other religions that people spoke about in those days. On the other hand, she was not a shaman, although she knew so much about it. Meanwhile she made little bags to keep nearly anything – for hunting, and also what was needed for the dead to take with them."

No one in the area was Christian then or now, but apparently people had heard of it, and Buddhism as well. During the Soviet period, of course, none of the religions were allowed, even shamanism, which is not strictly a religion in the eyes of many. Before the Soviet period, the Udege stayed with their own religions, with nature and spirits, and it was only the Russians who were Christian when the religion came back.

Auntie Dusia could certainly pray – anyone could. The little bags Polina mentions could be for anyone to use, but could especially be taken for the dead. Shamans could do the same. I'm not sure what was in it, but certainly small and important things – perhaps those that the dead people have always kept with themselves, like a knife or a pipe. Truly she was not a shaman – it just proved that other people could be very helpful too.

Polina sang for us, eyes bright, voice shining. Her song was about her uncle Jansi Kimonko, the first Udege writer, her mother's brother. She took after her mother, who was known for her singing – perhaps Auntie Dusia had written the song. We all enjoyed it.

How Shamans Worked in Those Days

Although Yevdokia Batovna was not a shaman herself, there were several in the village who were. She introduced us to the way shamans used to work before outsiders arrived. It was quite different from today, possibly because in the past people were more familiar with the shamans and what they have learned simply by watching. The terms "great and small" are the two levels of shaman we will see here. "Great" shamans speak of taking the dead to the next world, while "Small" shamans take care of other people in more ordinary situations. The spirits of their trees and waters stayed clearly with the people, and they treated these spirits with respect.

The Nanai people are good neighbours, living just to the north, but they do not always do things the way the Udege do. They have three levels of shamans instead of two: the first is a person who can do healing only for him or herself; the second is a person who can do healings and ceremonies for others; and the highest level, for both the Nanai and the Udege, is a shaman who conducts the dead to the next world. In this area, including Siberia, this is the most important fumction, although this is not the case for all shamans of the world.

I've heard that most shamans are seen at birth as being different from other children. For example, some are able to go out onto the ice with no clothing, while others understand unfamiliar languages. I've also heard these things of people in the north.

The words Auntie Dusia speaks may be tricky to follow in places. In reading them, we have to discern when the shaman is actually with people in the room and his spirit flying. Or is he negotiating with the Great-Grandmother? It's as if we were sometimes in the room and in other times we are in a dream. When is the child in the room and when is his soul elsewhere? Does the mother now speak from the room?

Perhaps such things are always hazy, as are parts of the story of Sister and Brother. Many younger people have reminded me that their elders told them that they were asking too many questions. We may be too, having been raised in a culture that frequently looks for logic rather than spirit. The next two examples show things that shamans can do. The work of a shaman – the healers of Siberia – was both honoured and feared by people who knew and watched them. Here is what Yevdokia Batovna said about it. Most of the major differences in the Shamanism came from outsiders.

A Shaman for a Child. Spoken by Yevdokia Batovna in Her Own Udege Language and Russian. Written in Translation into Russian by Valentina Kyalundzyuga

In the olden days, shamans were both great and small. Before the beginning of a *kamlanie*, a shamanic ceremony, they put on a shaman's white clothing. It had a frog and a terrifying snake or crocodile, called *singmu*, sewn onto it.[5] Above the belt there were red and black stripes, and the belt itself was made of hide, in the form of a snake with a stinger. Metal and lead bells were sewn onto the belt.

They put a horn made of wood onto the hat, and on the edge of it they made a frog and snake. There were either wooden or birchbark masks for the face, and stripes were also drawn on the mask. Trim was made with bear fur on all sides. Wood shavings were attached on the elbows and knees, as well as the head, the forehead, and also on the *uly*, the slippers.[6]

Starting his ceremony for a sick child, the shaman searches for the solution. He knows this child has no soul now. Before the shaman's ceremony, people make a nest out of skin called *omé*.[7] A woman would keep the spirits of her future children in the nest. Eyes are added from blue beads – it's a favourite colour. The *omé* is kept on a mythical tree named *khuigha*.

The child is very ill for a long, long time, and searches again for his soul. Only when he finds it will he get well. People bring a little tree with three branches from the mountain forest *taiga*. On these three branches they place a nest made of dried grasses and on the ends of these three branches they tie scraps of fabric. The shaman then begins to sing his *kamlanie*. He begins to sing quietly, moving his voice through his gut and then calling his helping spirit. Quietly he beats the drum, divining where the child's soul is now.

And, having found it, he speaks. "The soul of this child has gone back to his own nest." They will have to make a request for this soul from the Great Grandmother, *Sagdi Mama*. She is the one who takes care of a child's soul in the *omé*. Then she will send it to a living person – a woman who gives birth to the child. Great-Grandmother keeps an eye out to see that the child grows, that no one torments him, that he doesn't get ill and doesn't go hungry. If the child gets sick, she takes his soul back into the *omé* and puts him back onto the mythical *khuigha* tree.

In the form of his spirit-helper, the shaman sets off after the child's soul. His own soul flies over mountains and rivers. He gets close to the highest mountain and climbs up onto it. There, the shamanic spirit turns from a little bird into a caterpillar, and then a butterfly. Then it flies in such a way that Great-Grandmother will not see him. He flies and flies and turns into a very small butterfly. In the form of the spirit helper, he comes close to Great-Grandmother's *balagan*, a temporary place to live, sometimes a tent or a house. He flies around and around Great-Grandmother, and she waves her hands – that butterfly is bothering her!

She asks, "Who has come? If you've come with news, speak!"

The shaman begins to talk with Great-Grandmother.

"I have come for the soul of my child."

Great-Grandmother says, "Look after the child, so that he does not fall endlessly, and so that he gets no black and blue marks."

The shaman asks the child's mother, "Great-Grandmother asks why the child has a black and blue mark."

The mother replies, "He was playing and fell on the firewood."

Now she called to her child, using a word that is repeated in a song for the mother of a sick child. She sings, asking Great-Grandmother to return her child.

"*Dekhené, dekhené,*
Come back my son,
Dekhené, dekhené,
Come back to your mother.
Play with your toys,
Dekhené, dekhené,
Come back to your mother!
Come here and eat!
Dekhené, dekhené.

Great-Grandmother agrees to give the child back. The shaman puts the child's spirit into his own mouth and returns to the world of living people. He comes to the place where the live people are. The shaman blows the child's soul from his own mouth into the child's skin, *omé*. After that, they hang it on the *khuigha* tree. And after a certain time that *omé* is sewn into the child's clothing.

We listened another day and this time learned more about the next world. ▾

As I listened to these stories, I tried carefully to understand everything Yevdokia Batovna said. We sat in her house, on the low chairs so familiar to the Udege, drinking tea. I looked out the window, and then watched my recorder to make sure it was still working. She told the stories in both languages – giving me practice at picking up the Udege language a bit.

Later Valentina wrote the Russian part for me on brown paper, the kind that may deteriorate easily. Both of them gave me my permission to translate it into English.

A Shaman Carries the Dead to the Next World. Spoken by Yevdokia Batovna in Her Own Language and Russian

When someone is ill and dying, people call a shaman to carry the soul to the world beyond the grave. The soul of this sick person will not leave alone, and if the soul stays in our world for a long time, it will become an evil spirit. The relatives will get sick and die. For this reason, they say, "Take the dead quickly to the next world."[8]

On one specific day, the preparation takes place in the *balagan*, the tent. They make the form of a person out of dry grass and set it up with a stick at the back. In the tent many people are sitting quietly – very quietly. The shaman begins the ceremony, after putting on his robe, hat, and a special belt. In the *balagan* people burn *bagul'nik* – a ledum plant – and smoke comes from it.

The shaman begins to sing in his own voice – quietly, quietly, and then he sings and sings louder and louder. He beats the drum louder. When his helping spirit comes, he calls, "*sok sok sok sok*." This is a special sound for calling a helping spirit. After that, the shaman stands and begins to chant.

He continues, and finds the soul of the deceased person under the arm of his wife. And then the shaman makes her enter the *pudenka* – which is a receptacle that seems to be in the form of a person, made from grasses. After that he sits in the middle of the tent and sets up a feast before taking the soul to the next world. The shaman talks with the soul of that dead person, who then speaks to his wife and children so that they will live well. The dead one is given vodka, tobacco, and food.

When everything is over, they take the soul away. The shaman takes the sledge to the head of the river and from there into an opening in the mountain. The shaman ties the sledge and uses a skin strap as a belt. And the people in the room hold this strap so that the helping spirit of the shaman will not stay in the next world. He dives into an opening in the rock cliff and arrives at the country of the dead.

"In our world it is summer, and in theirs, winter – it's cold," he reports.

And all the same, he has to keep moving, as if walking on skis. He doesn't go for long when he sees the tracks of a sledge. In that place they live by their own laws. The shaman leaves the person's soul there and returns. All who are there in the *balagan* now bring the *pudenka* out. Returning, the shaman again goes through the opening. And, returning into this world, he orders his helpers to let go of the strap. With that he finishes his ceremony, and then people smoke, drink tea, or something else.

A month after seeing this soul off, drumming is arranged. Someone goes out to people living here and there, so they will know where the *gongoi* – the drumming – will take place.[9] Everyone gathers there. Shamans living up and down the river are called. In summer, many come on boats, quickly pushing off with poles. People come wearing their holiday clothing, with decorated robes. The shaman plays the drum sitting on the boat. People come from up and down the river. Many gather – it's fun! Here and there people set up tents. They make a fire and use a big cast-iron pot for preparing *lemé*. This food is boiled and cut from the fat under the skin of a deer, made in the form of a snake with stripes cut on it.

Before the shaman starts to beat his drum, it is played by ordinary people, not shamans. After that, the shaman begins to beat the drum. They burn *bagul'nik* for smudging, and the shaman quietly, quietly, begins to beat the drum. All helpers take bells and make sounds with them over the shaman's head. The shaman's spirit helper appears – the humpback spirit.

The helpers imitate having the hump themselves. The shaman sings in the voice of a hunchback.

When the hunchback finishes, they play a musical *ngasigdai*, a shaman's way of playing and calling. One person beats the drum with a rattle. Another person plays the same drum along with him, using two sticks. This person is not a shaman, but simply plays the drum. The third person plays the bells, while some play horns made of tree bark. Those who play this music call out to the spirit helper of the shaman. The fire is just one coal, the corners in pitch darkness now. The shaman beats the drum – boom boom boom! His loud voice rings out, while all around people sit quietly, quietly. All that is left to be heard is the shaman's singing. At last, he orders someone to shoot him with a bow and arrow, right into his chest. Here the shaman falls to the ground as if dead – a little shiver along his legs. He lies without moving. As soon as he begins to move his feet, people remove the arrow. They sprinkle a decoction of *bagul'nik*. He sits, pushing hot coals into his mouth, and blows so that sparks fly away, and walks barefoot on the coals. He chants. It's frightening for people to look at how the shaman does all this. The shaman's spirit flies, and he asks all the seated people where the spirit is flying.

People say, "He's flying on the hill."

"He flies over the source of the river."

He asks, "Where did he sit?"

People say, "He sat on a tree, from the side where the sun rises."

As soon as the ceremony ends, everyone eats *lemé* in the shape of a snake.

All come from here and there to one place, and they all celebrate. ▼

We'll learn more about more modern shamanism in chapter 5.

2

VALENTINA TUNSIANOVNA KYALUNDZYUGA

Spirituality, Storytelling, Education, and Work for All

Travelling through the forested mountains, we stopped at the top for Valentina Tunsianovna to speak with the spirits of the places. She asked them to give me health and a good trip home, and we gave some of our food as gifts to the mountain, sending our good will in both directions – one to the place we were leaving and the other we were entering. She spoke in the Udege language, of which I understood just enough to hear about the mountains and spirit.

She has a poetic turn of mind, which she uses frequently. Beliefs are strong, but Valentina Tunsianovna never pushes them onto others.

Alexander's car had stopped on a flat spot surrounded by such thick trees that I wouldn't have known that we had reached the top. It had arrived very gradually. When we got out of the car, my clothes got immediately muddy from the puddles that had splashed the doors. We ate our lunch of cheese and bread, sharing it with the spirits.

Valentina Tunsianovna Kyalundzyuga and I met in the late summer of 1993, introduced by her niece Nadezhda Efimovna Kimonko. Nadia and I had met at a festival on Sakhalin Island, and she convinced me that, if I came to Khabarovsk and the villages, she could introduce me to a lot of storytellers. That proved to be completely true. The first place she took me was to her favourite village, Gvasyugi, where she had lived in early childhood.

I soon met several very welcoming people in Gvasyugi. One was the storyteller Eofu Sisilievich Kimonko. We sat with him in a hut by the river – so small that we had to crawl in. His first story shocked me. It was about a cannibal god who stole a girl's tongue, and she died. Her sister found her tongue in the barn and brought both the tongue and her life back. This was only the beginning of stories very different from any I had ever heard, although I hadn't heard too many at that time. That was about to change, with women and men telling similar tales.

Next, we went on to see Valentina Tunsianovna. When the tea was ready, the stories came out. The first was about a clever contest between two shamans, and the next about a man who fell in love with a seal. There were layers and layers of meaning, and so it went. I was hooked.[1]

Over the next twelve years, we met again and again, usually in the village of Gvasyugi, but also in Yukon, in Vancouver, British Columbia, and in the city of Khabarovsk. We became friends, each of us having stayed in the other's home by then. We worked on a book together, and I told many of her stories to Canadians, who needed explanations, as I had at the beginning. After a while, the oddity of Eofu Kimono and his stories had become normal.

Here is one of Valentina's favourites from ancient times. It can always remind us of difficult times and how people succeed courageously in them. She found Zabini Nyambyevna Kyalundzyuga at some point after 1960, while gathering stories that she kept in a notebook. At that time, no one was recording. Valentina had a notebook with facing pages – Udege on one side and Russian on the other. She decided which story to tell that day.

Two Suns. From Udege and Their Indigenous Storytellers. Told by Zabini Nyambyevna Kyalundzyuga, Born in 1909 in Lazo Region

There lived one hunter, Yegdiga, with his wife. At that time there were two suns that shone very hot. The trees and grasses dried up, and the water in the river dried up. Animals and birds ran away. There was nothing in the *taiga* forest to breathe. The children of Yegdiga were born and died. He was angry, made arrows, and set off.

The two suns did not rise far up – they stood over the highest rock cliff. When once they went up over the cliff, Yegdiga shot from his bow and spoke, "Bow, aim right into the sun! You have always helped me in difficult moments. Help me now in this very tough time!" The arrow flew with a noise, the land itself was turning over. It hit right into one of the suns and that one got very dim. The other sun rose up.

Since that time there has been just one sun in the world, and one moon. The world became joyous, the trees and grasses grew again. The animals and birds came back. They made their sounds and sang to themselves. And the water ran murmuring in the river with shoal after shoal at each bend. This is how they began to live. ▾

Interestingly, this story is heard in much of Asia, with various numbers of suns. Valentina was interested to hear this one from the Indigenous people of Taiwan. I had heard it while sharing stories in Vancouver.

We enjoyed looking at the two stories one after the other to see their different details, as storytellers always do.

I saw a Russian book of Valentina Kyalundzyuga's at her home, which unfortunately has lately burned. It showed not just Two Suns but also Seven Suns in the whole area, and perhaps more. I have not seen them again.

Two Suns. From Taiwan and Their Indigenous Storytellers. Told in Vancouver, British Columbia, by the Taiwanese Storyteller Francis Wong. He Translated It into English

Long ago there were neither moon nor stars. When the sun set, everything was completely dark. There was nothing to do.

Time passed, and the sun seemed closer. It was very bright and hot. The sun seemed closer – even more bright and hot. People looked up and suddenly understood that there were two suns in the sky.

Then it became too hot; no one could work. Trees, flowers, and grasses dried up, and there was no water in the rivers.

There was also no more food for people or their animals.

The old people worried. They called a gathering. People talked and finally they decided to send three young men who might shoot the second sun from the sky.

Each of them took with him a baby, because they knew that this trip would be very long. They went past mountains and forests, met wild animals, and fought with them.

They brought fruit seeds and planted them, so that later the trees could show them the road home.

Day after day they walked, while the young men turned into old men. Their three children grew up and learned from their fathers the arts of hunting, fishing, and shooting from a bow and arrow.

At last, they saw the second sun – very close. It was so bright that they had to cover their eyes. They shot! The flame of that sun got weaker and turned into a small circle – the moon. The other flame became stars. Now everything was normal.

The three young heroes returned, and spent much time around the fruit trees. Delicious! When they got home, their hair was already grey. ▼

Memories

I have many memories of time spent with my friends, some humorous, such as the time we went into a Russian publisher's office in Khabarovsk to pick up copies of one of our books. This time we had worked together stories in three languages – Udege, Russian, and English. The book contained several folk tales for children. The publisher had worked for Valentina many times before, and appreciated her work, but this time he seemed unable to find the copies, and he disappeared from his office for a long time, perhaps checking the Internet.

Finally, Valentina Tunsianovna took things in hand, and looked around. "After all," she said, "we have rights to a fair number of copies." And besides, a car and driver were waiting outside to take us first to Gvasyugi and then to Krasny Yar. It was a long way.

All three of us found cartons with our books in a different room, and helped ourselves; then off to our waiting car. We were able to distribute the books to schools and to some officials – and even a few copies for Canadian libraries. As far as I know there was no comment from the publisher.

By 2005, I had visited several other places in Russia and had friends there as well, but I always passed through Khabarovsk, since at that time it was the first stop along the way in either direction. In the nineties, there was an Aeroflot flight direct from Khabarovsk to Anchorage and beyond, through Seattle. However, later only one Russian plane was used for this international flight, and it got worse and worse. Many Russian planes were like that at that time. In fact, most were not well kept – or at all. This one made so much noise over Alaska and Canada that people who lived below complained, afraid that it would fall on them. After that the flight was no longer permitted. Imagine what the noise was like inside the plane! It was terrifying. Safety concerns were raised by the noise, and these were important for Canada and the United States.

Alaska Airlines is, of course, much better, but the flight to Khabarovsk worked only for a few years. After that the trip took a longer route via Korea, and still does. And it is more expensive.

Once in Gvasyugi, I always found the village full of friendly people, and met others up and down the rivers. Unfortunately, though, after 2005, for personal reasons, I was not able to travel, and others could not come to me. We were only occasionally in touch.

Still, I kept thinking of them and of life in the villages, including the sounds of Valentina's music. Then, in 2018, I was given an award from Storytellers of Canada, our national organization. It was called "Storykeeper," a simple award, and endearing. I thought about people who had taught me to be a storykeeper – not just telling the tales but finding and keeping them alive somehow. I decided to speak about two people who had taught me the most: one of them was Valentina Kyalundzyuga and the other was Louise LeBlanc, born and raised as one of the Indigenous peoples of the Yukon. She had started an excellent storytelling festival, where I first met both people from our own north and from the Russian Far East. This had made the rest possible.

I spoke in the darkened room about Valentina Tunsianovna's large heart and the pleasures we had shared while riding the river in a boat. More pictures appeared – fishing, picnics, and entertaining an elder shaman, Adikhini, who pretended to be terrified in the boat. Each of us took a try at her drum, which turned out to be more difficult than I had imagined. We had to dance at the same time, with bells on our belts.

It came to me that I must go to Russia and see Valentina again. And so it was.

Finally, we arrived at the place I had most wanted to revisit, eager to see her. Gvasyugi was a well-settled and busy village in 2019, minus the *kolkhoz*, the collective farm where Auntie Dusia had worked long ago. Today, children can be seen walking to school and parents fishing, and everyone crosses the high bridge with no fear. Even today though, getting to Gvasyugi is a long, bumpy ride from the regional centre. But going by water would be longer and possibly more difficult.

In Gvasyugi, we got out of the car that had rattled along for hours. Nadia started to prepare lunch in the borrowed house where we would stay. At this time, Valentina had only a small room in a different house, since her own house had burned down some time ago. She would come to see us soon. Our driver, Alex, was as ready for a walk as I was, and we decided to cross over the frightening, but beautiful, new bridge. The old one had been right on the water, and your feet generally got wet, whereas the new one is high up and solid, but has no rails. On the other side, we walked a bit further to a larger river, the Khor. The way it moved had a magical sound, with chunks of ice moving quickly in the river like gentle, broken glass. We watched and listened a long time as Alex, also a photographer, took a video. Trees all around were gentle in the wind. Finally hungry, we returned to the house.

At last, I had a joyous reunion with Valentina. First we were shy, and then there was laughter, food, and gifts. Among other things, I had brought a small wooden box full of colourful pebbles from the beach in Vancouver. The box had a picture of a Canadian moose that had strongly drawn me. Now Valentina Tunsianovna told me she came from the elk clan, and was pleased that they were similar. She returned with a picture of a tiger, which now hangs on my wall, equally meaningful.

What is it that holds so many people to Valentina Tunsianovna? I had felt it as spirituality from the start, and was pulled back over many time zones to return. People who know her are equally amazed by her many works, and her great kindness and intelligence. Children who learned with her grew with great self-confidence. I still met such confident children in 2019, and it was a great pleasure on the street and in the school. She brings gifts to the peak of a mountain while travelling, and also puts a bear skull in a tree beside her house, so that the bears will feel comfortable there. She doesn't ask others to do the same, but does welcome us into her culture.

She has warmed many in Europe, Canada, and many parts of Russia, and, most of all, the people of her own village. Her stories can be dramatic.

One of her favourites is "Lugi Belye." She told this story at my request, since I knew that she loved it. We sat on easy chairs in the village. It was wonderful to be with a storyteller again, as Nadia and I had done so often in other years. Many of the elders were gone now, but Valentina Tunsianovna was going strong.

I had questions and asked for a story that is timely for both of our countries, with large forests plagued by fires in summer. But who is she? *Lugi* means roughly "Fiery." She personifies the element of forest fire bringing the land down. But *Belye* is a story word for a good woman; she appears in many stories.

"Is Lugi Belye both good and bad?" I asked. "Isn't fire like that?"

"Oh yes," she replied, as if that were just too obvious. "There is power in Lugi Belye, but more important is the power of the work that people do." She also mentioned that the other women in the story represent various shamans. Only they can obstruct and defeat Lugi Belye.

Here I appreciate the storyteller at the top of the following story, Igry Gaikalyevich. He told this story while people sat together in Gvasyugi, organized by Valentina Tunsianovna. The same will be true for the storytellers of most stories in this book, and I appreciate being allowed to translate them into English.

Lugi Belye, The Essence of Fire. Told to Valentina Kyalundzyuga by Igry Gaikalyevich Kyalundzyuga in the Years between 1960 and 1980 in Lazo Region

Yegdiga[2] lived in the *taiga*. Once he found out that a blazing young woman had appeared in the *taiga*. She was Lugi Belye. Wherever she walked, nothing grew; whoever she met, died. And no one could defeat her.

Yegdiga knew that to help he must take to the road, and so he got ready. He made two arrows, one of steel and the other of elk bone. He walked and walked along the banks of the river below, along the flow where the river became wider. And then he came to the mouth of the river, where it fell into the sea. Yegdiga walked along the sand, and there on the shore he saw Lugi Belye in the distance. She appeared, all blazing red. Where she appeared, everything burned with fire. The trees, and the grasses – all burned with bright, strong flames.

Lugi Belye came toward Yegdiga. She walked, magnificent with heat, coming right at him. Yegdiga took his arrow made of moose bone and shot at Lugi Belye. It hit her right in the heart, but it didn't bother her a bit. All that was left from the arrow was ash. Again, he shot, with his steel arrow. It fell right on Lugi Belye's heart and the steel arrow melted.

Lugi Belye chased after Yegdiga as he began to run. He ran and ran – ran and ran. He ran so much that he didn't know how much. Then he saw a tent, a *balagan*. A lovely young woman lived there, a shaman.

"Belye, get ready!" he called. "Lugi Belye is right after me."

Yegdiga hurried her. She gathered herself quickly, and the two of them ran together.

They ran and ran. Belye got tired, and Yegdiga started helping her so she wouldn't fall behind.

"Run alone, Yegdiga. I can't go any further," said Belye. "I will hold Lugi Belye down for a bit. On the road you will meet a tall man made of lead. Tell everything to this man. Then, on the road, you will meet a very large man made of iron. Tell this man that Lugi Belye is coming right after you. Farther along the road you will meet a woman – one of us. She will tell you what to do next."

Belye had just finished saying this to Yegdiga when Lugi Belye appeared. She was running, and fiery sparks were carried by the wind in all directions. Behind her, everything was burning.

"Run fast, Yegdiga! I am holding her with my shamanic power," said Belye.

Yegdiga began running. He ran and ran. And then he met a very large person made of lead. Yegdiga looked up. In comparison with that man, he was like a small bird.

"Man of lead, help! Lugi Belye is coming after me."

No sooner had Yegdiga spoken, when Lugi Belye appeared. Her long hair was flying in all directions, sparks flew from her nose and eyes in the wind. Lugi Belye glowed on everything. She ran strongly. The man of lead blocked Lugi Belye's way, and Yegdiga ran further. But not for long did the lead man block her way. He melted, and all that was left of him was a small, small mound.

Yegdiga ran and ran. He ran and met a very large iron man. He was just as big as the lead man. Beside this iron man, Yegdiga was the size of a grasshopper.

"Iron man, help! Lugi Belye is coming after me!" Yegdiga prayed.

He had just spoken, when Lugi Belye showed up. The iron man blocked the road, and Yegdiga ran onward. He did not stop. But the iron man also melted, and all that was left of him was a small mound.

Yegdiga ran further with all his strength. He ran and saw a tent – a *balagan* – where another Belye lived.

"Belye, Lugi Belye is coming after me," called Yegdiga. "Let's run together!"

"Yegdiga, I will go to meet Lugi Belye. I know it will be a difficult, heavy fight before us," said the second Belye.

She put on her belt and put on her robe.

"You sit in the tent. When I come back, I myself will say what we must do next." And she went out.

The sky was black, and the wind strong. The sun had disappeared. But after a little while, outside you could hear the noise getting less – the heavens became tarnished, and the sun began to seem crimson.

He listened, and all became calm. Again, all around there was light, the sun shone and the wind dispelled the smoke. Belye came and collapsed on a bear skin. She spoke in a barely audible voice.

"Yegdiga, now it's your turn. Go and search for a stone cliff. On the shore of the river, you'll find a cliff of strong rock. On the top of this cliff there is a golden *balagan*. In that tent lives a golden rabbit. Getting up this cliff is not easy though."

She spoke these words and then was silent.

He knew that a golden rabbit was a healer.

Yegdiga set off. He took hemp rope measuring seven thousand wheel *sazhens*, and started searching for the stone cliff.[3] And where was it? He didn't know. Along the road he saw the cliff. From that cliff came light – the kind that, when you look at it, it darkens your outlook. Yegdiga hit himself on the head and turned into a centipede. He crawled the cliff and crawled to get to the top of the cliff, and there saw a golden tent. At the door, he turned back into Yegdiga.

The golden rabbit suddenly saw him and was frightened.

"Yegdiga, I knew that you would come out of your *balagan*. I recognized the way you walked. But I didn't know that you would come up here. No one can come up to the top of this cliff. Everyone who wanted to come up – their bones lie at the bottom of the cliff. It should have been that way with you, and yet you have defeated me. But before you take hold of me, allow me to jump around the tent."

The rabbit ran several times, jumped, around the *balagan*, leapt up, and flew into the sky. Yegdiga threw his rope measuring seven thousand wheel *sazhens* at the rabbit. The rope made a ball and fell back down to the earth, along with the rabbit. Yegdiga held the other end in his hand.

He set off, back to Belye, taking his rabbit. He arrived, killed it, and, without spilling a single drop of blood on the earth, he filled a birchbark basket with it. He spread Belye's body with blood rubbed everywhere.

Belye opened her eyes. Her cheeks and lips glowed again. Yegdiga was joyful that he had saved his Belye, the woman who feared nothing. She loved a man who would work so hard to bring her healing. They married and began to live well.[4] ▼

Valentina's Early Life

Valentina Tunsianovna Kimonko (as she was named before her marriage) was born in 1936 to a family of hunter-fisher people in a nomad camp on the river Sukpai. The camp was near the town of Chuken, not far from Gvasyugi. Her family consisted of her mother, Apchi, and her father, Tunsiana Chingesovich Kimonko, several brothers and sisters, and Valentina herself.

Her father descended from ancient hunters by the name of Kimonko. He said that, far back, the Udege lived on the shore by the Sea of Japan. They had to move, searching for a better place, because of a cataclysm and hunger.

The family lived in a *Kava*, a small house made of tree bark. It was cold in there, and in winter, from a very young age, Valentina started to work. She kept the fire going while her mother and father went out hunting. As a four-year-old girl, she kept firewood continuously in the stove, so they would not freeze there in the mountainous Sikhote-Aline *taiga*. She also helped her mother making clothing and shoes from animal and fish skins.

Music

In the Udege world, music includes much more than we may think. It belongs not only to people, but to animals, spirits, and even ritual objects. Valentina Tunsianovna sings now as her mother did, both lyric melodies and music that goes with storytelling. She says that spirits can be heard only by shamans, but that we can hear something that connects us with those spirits while hearing stories. Certainly, music and story belong together in a sacred place.

It fascinates me to hear that it's not just people who are understood as real musicians, but also animals, birds, and even musical instruments. I have played the cello for most of my life, and I agree that the instrument is alive as long as it is played regularly. The music livens the wood. It all makes sense when we listen and pay attention, slowing down to hear in a new way.

My own love of melodies and instruments goes back to my parents, who both played the piano. Our neighbour taught me the cello – one of the many instruments that changes along with the weather. We lived on the outskirts of a small town, where there were more birds singing than people. And now, while I walk in a big-city park in pouring rain, the sound on the umbrella helps to dampen car noise. No wonder Valentina's songs come so easily around the rivers, birds, wind, and rain.

For the Udege, music can be played with heroes who embody magical movement, as well as shamans helping the dead to the next world. Musicians may be acting out emotions of all sorts, as part of a performance or a shamanic ceremony. They may also play for children, along with telling stories. Each melody has its own meaning. Hunters often learn the voices of birds and animals, singing to attract them.[5]

Udege people often hold certain notes longer while singing. They sustained them longer while singing than when they were speaking. I've heard Valentina Tunsianovna sing on the river with only two or three notes. Her notes went back and forth with c-d-a – all moving upward. Later she sang the song-story "Kilae," with notes alternating up and down, d-f-d-c. The scholar Yuri I. Sheikhin finds more, including: e-d-c-e-g, and c-d-g-f-g, while one man I heard told a whole story singing on only two notes.

Mother's Stories

Over the years, Valentina Tunsianovna kept a clear image of her mother telling her stories before she went to sleep. "She got tired during the day and, all the same, I would ask her for a story and she would sing one each time." The daughter still performs some of these tales dramatically – the big roaring bear, the bird rising high and laughing.

Valentina loved to run in the mountains and trees, gathering berries, looking at wild animals and creeks. She grew to be a hunter, as was her mother, along with many Udege women. Her favourite grandmother told the *nimonku*, a type of magical story that often had its beginning in a dream of the storyteller or ancestor. Nadia's grandmother told the same kind of stories. Valentina was always eager for evening to hear grandmother's melodious voice telling the adventures of the great hunter Yegdiga and the talented, beautiful Belye – as well as a scary and smart monster.

"Most likely every one of us would like to have such a mother and grandmother, so kind and wise," Valentina recalls.

Around the time when her grandmothers were alive, there were book burnings in many parts of Russia. I heard this from the historian Valentin Ilych Geiker years ago. He showed me the very place where all books printed in the Latin alphabet were burned outside the houses in a village just up the Amur River from Khabarovsk.

This happened throughout the Soviet Union in 1930, when the government changed the alphabet from the Latin, like ours, to Cyrillic, which is Russian. This change was undoubtedly a setback in the beginning for those who were just learning, and then had to start over. On the other hand, it helped the students to learn only one alphabet, and got stronger with their work. Of course, all of this was still before Valentina's birth.

School

Valentina Tunsianovna started school in 1944, and she loved the Russian stories as well as their own, often sitting by a kerosene lamp to read.

It was Nadezhda who told me about the first schools that arrived in the Udege area in the 1930s, although I understand the Russian educators had begun elsewhere earlier in the 1920s. Male teachers from either Leningrad or Khabarovsk would gather the children of the nomad camps and teach them to read. Gradually they organized huts and read to both children and grown-ups, thus teaching the Indigenous people of all ages. As a result, the Udege moved from nomad camps into a new kind of settlement, where there was a school, a store, and a few other establishments.

Nadia says that, thanks to the teachers' selflessness, the school became an authoritative organization in the village. The town that became Gvasyugi started to be developed around that time. The school was established to teach children the Russian language, since most of the Udege did not speak it at the time. A *kolkhoz* – a common farm – was also established.

Nadia also says that, in the 1930s, those Russian teachers were able to infuse the love of education into people. At first, they taught only those eight to seventeen years old in the Udege language. I have wondered how these Russian teachers learned the Udege language – or did they teach Russian without it, as many teach students from various countries that speak languages the teacher does not understand?

Valentina grew up later than that, given she was born in 1936, although her family was still in the forest camps at that time. They didn't want to go to a village, but at last moved, later than others, so that their children could go to school there. It was not all their choice.

The Soviet Government

The Soviets had arrived in some areas as early as the 1920s, hoping to move more people out of the forests. Some managed to stay in the woods, but with time more and more arrived in the villages. By about 1940, Valentina's family were moved forcibly by the Soviets, although they had managed to evade them for a long time.

In fact, some people stayed in the forests throughout the far east of Siberia and Russia for many years more, and perhaps are there even now.

Theoretically, this move to the village should have improved the families' lives, but, in spite of some benefits, in reality they lost their former territory. The land now had only nine small settlements in a large territory – and they were still isolated. In the second quarter of the last century, the only transportion artery was the Khor River.

In the thirties through the forties, several adult Udege went to study in the new *Институт Народов Севера* (Institute of the Peoples of the North) in Leningrad, as St Petersburg was known at the time. It prepared northern minorities to teach in boarding schools, and also created a research institute. I've heard that, along with their education, the students benefited greatly from knowing young people from other parts of the country. All of them spoke Russian, and most also spoke their own languages. After they graduated, they began to teach in their own villages.

Gradually, the new ways of education and living took over. The students learned to sleep on beds and to use furniture and dishes different from those in their homes, since they had often slept and eaten on the floor. Learning was useful, although many schools had poor supplies of schoolbooks and other things. But, in spite of the problems, the children received a free education. Many went on to specialized and higher education in the regional centres and in the city of Khabarovsk.

In Soviet times, it was typical that students would receive the beginning and middle of their educations, and either vocational or higher education, in larger towns. There was support from the government: free living in a dormitory when needed, free outer winter and fall clothing, footgear, a stipend, and vouchers for the dining room.

Valentina grew up in the latter part of this system. The Udege youth turned out to be very intelligent, and did well. "I speak not just of my friends, but many others," Nadia insists.

Of course, the education I've described here did not necessarily work in other parts of Russia, or even necessarily very far from these villages. The *gulags*, or prison camps, struck terror into the whole country for at least the years from 1918 to 1960 under Lenin and Stalin and beyond. Millions suffered and died as they worked with no pay, inadequate clothing and housing, and little food. The camps are still shown in museums as a great shame for the country.

Nadezhda says about the gulag: "I heard from my grandfather. He said that one of the Udege in the village was an informer. I don't remember the name and surname. Several people were in prison for contacting the Japanese [in the Second World War]. And many men, including the writer Jansi Kimonko, my grandfather Yengili Kimonko, and others, having learned that people were being put in jail, fled to the remote *taiga* to save their lives.

After seven years of education, Valentina Tunsianovna went to a pedagogical institute outside Khabarovsk to the north. There she met with others, and remembers the following years as some of her best times. She loved mathematics in particular, and things she learned then are useful now when helping her grandchildren. She loved to learn, but she got ill at one point and had to return home, where she recovered well.

There, she worked doing accounting in the village council and then became manager of the village club. She started going around the houses, inviting people to "Evenings for Elders," such as the evenings Igry Kyalundzyuga attended. He was the one who told the story of "Lugi Belye," and they all enjoyed it. Not only did they talk about their own lives, so that younger people could hear and understand, but they spoke in the voices and intonation of the characters in their stories. There were memories, tales, legends, and songs. It was then that Valentina decided to write them down and keep them, seeing the importance of their own culture, as well as the Russian. I remember a beaten-up notebook, where she had recorded the stories in two languages, on facing pages – one side Udege and the other Russian. She would page through them, deciding which stories to tell me, and then set the book down, since she knew them all by heart.

In the beginning of the 1960s, the people put together a folklore ensemble, with dance and music. They had help from a leader in Leningrad, which may explain the dance styles that so often were seen by foreigners as a kind of ballet. The group started little by little to perform farther away – first in the territory, then nationally, and even in Europe.

They also worked with art, including a circle for sewing and embroidery, taught by elders. The women were very powerful in organizing things, as they always have been. The men performed very well too, although they were also busy with other things, such as fishing and hunting.

Valentina Tunsianovna married and had several children, including Onisia, who also became an excellent storyteller. It seems now that communism had some very good points when it was in the right hands.

In 1968, Valentina was chosen chair of the executive committee of Gvasyugi's area, where she worked for thirty years. From 1992 to 1998, she was head administrator within the village. New houses and a new school building were put together. The people were careful to keep the forest and the Chechen basin safe around them.

At the end of the 1980s, a foreign company wanted to cut the forest around the village. Gathering the council, Valentina wrote to the High Council of the Soviet Union. A commission came all the way from Moscow to inspect the situation, agreeing that the area would be preserved. It became the Chechen reserve, and the right of the Udege to keep their traditional way of life was secured.

From her early years, Valentina continued to write. In 1974, her children's book, *Два Солнца* (*Two Suns*), came out. Design was by the brilliant artist Gennadi Pavlishin. He lives in Khabarovsk and has studied the culture deeply. All of his characters represent actual people, wearing the real-life clothing of the Udege, Nanai, and others. Pavlishin's books can be found in many houses, since he shows real members of the families. That endears him to his readers, and the delightful borders he has drawn make them perfect.

Because of her health, Valentina had to retire in 1998. But this did not stop her. She worked on books with M.D. Simonov, an excellent linguist specializing in the Udege language. He was the one who said that she had a poetic turn of mind, which she uses frequently. He lived and worked in the city of Novosibirsk, but made several visits to Gvasyugi and remained a dear friend. They co-authored a three-volume Udege-Russian dictionary, with fascinating and often long explanations. Next, in the same year, came another bilingual book in the series, *Памятники Фольклора Народов Сибири и Дальнего Востока. Фольклор, Удэгейцев, Ниманку, Тэлунгу, Ехэ* (*Monuments of Folklore of the Peoples of Siberia and the Far East: Folklore, Udege, Telengu, Ekhe*). This is the book, full of stories, biographies, explanations, songs, and unique words, from which I have learned the most. She also created an ABC book for young children.

She became head of the national trade commune "Ude," and assistant head of the regional section of the Russian Association of Indigenous Peoples of the North, known as RAIPON. She headed the Udege national folklore dance ensemble, *Су Гакпай* (Rays of Sun). In 2003, she was awarded the prize of *Душа Россий* (Soul of Russia), in the category of *Народный Рассказчик* (Folk Storyteller), from the Ministry of Culture of the Russian Federation. She won the Laureate prize from the governor of Khabarovsk Territory in the area of folk-art creativity, and is a member of the Writers' Union of Russia. There is more – Russia has many awards. However, in spite of all her prolific work, she remains very modest.

More recently, Valentina Kyalundzyuga and Nadezhda Kimonko worked hard on a fascinating book called *Мир Хозяина Воды Лунгиэ* (*The World, Master of Water Called Lungie*), a fine mix of science and storytelling, as we will see in the next chapter. The two have collaborated many times with their ideas, in their village and in the city.

Indigenous people have undergone periods of difficult transformation during Valentina Tunsianovna's years. Russian culture now predominates – including in language, literature, films, and television. On a larger scale, globalization is experienced all over the world, including that of disease and racism. The Udege have responded in various ways, some by moving to the city and beyond. Others have stayed in the village, becoming bilingual and bringing many cultural events out to their neighbours. Some find today's world exciting, and others are distressed by it – like people everywhere. Valentina Tunsianovna rides the wave well. She keeps her beliefs, while talking on her cellphone.

When we were in Gvasyugi, we stayed in a house with a dog tied up outdoors. That dog barked all the time and was quite annoying. In general, people have dogs only to be practical, not as a part of the family, and never in their houses. But in the following story, we can understand that dogs are really very helpful and kind – a sentiment shared by the Udege.

Guasa, a Good Dog. Told by Valentina Kyalyundzyuga in Her Book *Two Suns*

A woman named Agdenka had a son she called Kicho and a dog named Guasa.

Agdenka softened skins so diligently that her scraper got broken. There was nothing she could do, and she asked her dog to go up on the seven mountains. "Ask Yegdige Vai to come and fix it," she said.

Next day, just at early light, the dog named Guasa ran to find Yegdige Vai. She ran to the seven mountains, and saw one yurt there. Before going in, the dog went around the house and saw bones everywhere. "My mistress could not do better than Yegdige Vai, no matter how dangerous," she thought, and went in. "Vai, my mistress sent me and asked that you repair her scraper."

Vai agreed and said he would come at midday.

The dog ran home and told it all to Agdenka. "Yegdige Vai is a robber – and beside that, his yurt has bones scattered around!" she said. They were afraid and began to think how to save themselves, forgetting all about the scraper. They gathered everything and readied the sledge, so they could get away. Sure enough, Vai came at midday, as promised.

Earlier Agdenka had prepared bellows behind the hut. Vai started to forge, and Guasa fanned the bellows. Agdenka quickly put her son Kicho in the sledge.

Vai worked a little, and then asked for lunch. Guasa ran to Agdenka again. "He wants you to make lunch for him."

Agdenka asked of Heaven, "Send us tasty fat for the robber's lunch ... if we stay alive –" Her words were not yet finished when some fat fell from heaven. She quickly prepared lunch, called Vai to eat, and gave him the food. Then she got on the sledge with the dog and child.

"Run as fast as you can," she called. "We'll go away from the robber." The dog ran as fast as possible. But they saw Vai catching up.

"Guasa, stop! I want to get out. I can't go any more," said Agdenka at last.

"Hold on. We'll stop in a while. But now, Vai would kill us," said Guasa, and continued running.

They ran and ran. Suddenly the running got easier. Agdenka had fallen from the sledge and Guasa didn't stop. The dog ran and ran, the weather got worse and worse as the wind was wailing. A storm came up, darker and darker. But Guasa ran with the small child, Kicho. At last the wind got less, everything lightened. They had run away from Vai. Dog Guasa made a tent of straw and began to feed the child and live with him. He hunted for goat and rabbit.

One time there was nothing to eat. Guasa said, "Kicho, don't go far – wait for me." The dog went. She walked and walked and walked, on the track of a hunter who was carrying heavy things. Guasa caught up – the hunter had meat and the bag was full! Then after a bit it was easier for the hunter to carry the heavy sledge. He looked carefully and finally saw the dog.

Guasa worked hard, and ran even faster while the hunter slowed down. The wind blew, a storm came, the hunter lost sight of the dog. Guasa returned toward the tent where she and Kicho ate the meat!

The boy grew big, and learned to shoot the arrow. The young hunter brought home a bird and a squirrel.

Once Guasa said, "Don't go far, wait for me. I will try to return fast and bring you a bride."

Guasa ran down along the flow of the river, and then came to a hut. There lived old man Kanda Mafa and his wife, with their daughter, Ayaula. They never let their beloved daughter out, so that she would not get dark from the sun. On this day though, Ayaula wanted to go out.

"Let me outdoors, I want to watch the little sun, just standing beside a tree."

And so the old man and his wife covered their daughter with an eagle tail over her lovely face. She went out on the bank, and there she saw the dog Guasa.

"My father and mother did not let me out before," she said. "Here it is so light, there's no smell of smoke. Sitting in a hut is sad. I see only a little piece of sky across the smoke-hole … And a dog is good," said Belye Ayaula.

She called, "Father and mother, I want to ride on a sledge. Harness this dog; let me ride!"

The old man and woman harnessed the dog, sat Ayaula up, and Guasa began running. She started along the road beside the old people, and then ran far from them. The old man and woman were cold and went to get warm in the yurt. The dog ran beside the sledge with Belye Ayaula. She ran and ran, the wind blew, a storm came up, day turned to night, and dog Guasa kept running. Finally, the wind receded, and the sky got light.

At sundown the dog ran to her own tent. After that, Kicho and Ayaula grew up together and, when the time came, they married. Kicho began to hunt and brought meat home. The dog Guasa just lay down on the other side of the tent and warmed her back – and got old.

One day she said, "Kicho and Ayaula, soon I will die. I've become old. Bury me in a good high place. After seven days come to my grave and dig up my head. Give the old man and woman whatever you find."

So the dog spoke, and then she died. Kicho grieved for his beloved dog. They buried her on the high place, as she had asked. After seven days they came to the grave. They dug beside her head and found gold and silver there. They took it to Belye's parents, gave them what they had found, and returned back to living in their own tent by the place they had buried the faithful dog Guasa. ▼

Valentina's Museum. Everything from Books and Embroidery to a Shaman's Mask

Valentina Tunsianovna began her museum in the 1990s. I remembered two huts and a barn outdoors and a small bookcase indoors, with about four books on it. When I came in 2019, the same outdoor buildings were still in place, while indoors a whole schoolroom was packed with pictures of local people honoured from the Second World War, books, and a map showing places the Udege lived long ago. Newer photos show Valentina's visit to the Yukon with Nadezhda and me. I was thrilled to see a copy of my own book, *The Flying Tiger*.

There is a very unusual shaman's coat. It's simple, with several kinds of spirits painted on it – frogs, rabbits, birds, lizards, and a snake. Beside the robe there is shaman's mask of wood – very rare. Even the Khabarovsk Regional Museum currently shows only one of them, and that one is only pictured in a book.[6]

I've heard that the masks are a connection with a shaman's ancestors and their skulls. Valentina Tunsianovna says the mask is called *sama begbini*, meaning in Udege "the shaman's face."

One wall is full of embroidery and explanations on how the work is done. I've always enjoyed the unique embroidery of the Udege masters. Their style is very different from those of their neighbours, such as the Nanai and others. Each Udege design is made from colourful silk embroidery threads that stand up a little from the fabric. The artist has first made a design with fish skin and covered it with threads. These designs often represent everything from sacred tigers to the dragon, master of thunder. There are magpies, creators of life on earth, and elks, masters of the cosmos. People wear embroidery, especially around openings, such as at the neck, around the wrists, and at the bottom of a dress or shirt, to keep evil spirits away. The back is especially important in protecting people from spirits, since we can't watch our backs. One robe Nadia and I saw in Naikhin had several colours of fish skin, generally made from one kind of salmon. This one was especially dramatic and difficult to make. It used several fish, but it would last many years.

While looking around Valentina Tunsianovna's museum, I brought up a question I'd been holding for years. At a conference that we had all attended, I'd heard people speak of different ways various people could communicate with spirits – by speaking or singing. For years I wanted to know how it worked for the Udege, since the various peoples had different ways. When I finally had the opportunity to ask Valentina Tunsianovna, the answer was a surprise. "It's a communication for shamans and spirits. They sing, but only shamans can hear it." But, she added, "Singing can also be for a storytelling, depending on the story or listeners."

What the Udege Believe In. Masters of Land, Water, and Fire. Explained by Valentina Tunsianovna as She Heard It from Michina Dulyevich Kimonko, Who Lived from 1902 to 1985

People believe that everything living, everything in the *taiga*, has its own masters: the land, water, and fire. People will do nothing bad to any of them. Numerous spirit-masters are connected with health.

One is *Khutakta*, the morning star, which comes up at sunrise. People turn to her for a good deed when others are ill. They burn *bagul'nik*, a plant used for many ceremonies, and throw food into the fire.

The Spirit-master of the earth lives in a rotten, fallen tree, which is never to be cut or accidentally touched, since that would offend the master. The offender's arm and leg would swell up, and finally the offender would ask for a blessing from the spirit-master.[7]

The Spirit-master of the water is also in a rotten tree, lying down. Fishermen always shared any food they had with the Spirit-master of water, who would then help them get fish. If a person's arm or leg swells, they say it has been called out by the Spirit-master of water and say that, if they heal the arm or leg, they are also healing the spirit-master.

Lungé (aka *Lungiye*) is one of the Spirit-masters of water. People pray to *Lungé* to give blessing in time of a strong flood. They burn *bagul'nik* and pray right at the water, asking *Lungé* to give a blessing when ice begins drifting, and trees fall as earth falls by the shore.

The Spirit-master of fire lives in the hearth, where there is a campfire. He is always around a person who is involved in preparing food. They give offerings to the Spirit-master of fire, so that there will always be animals and furs. It is forbidden to poke the fire with a sharp knife, since it might accidentally wound the spirit-master.

As soon as the Swan star comes at night, a very old man will ask her to give a blessing for any living people who suddenly got sick from an epidemic and died. The people also burn *bagul'nik*, and kill a rooster.

Every river has its own master. At the head of Sukpai, on the mountain cliff, there is a place where the Kimonko clan prayed. ▾

I've tried to find out about the Swan star and heard that it comes on a a certain day of the year. It was said to be wonderful in the village at night, since there was little light. But I'm still not sure which one it is!

3

NADEZHDA EFIMOVNA KIMONKO

Care for Youth; Research and Science; Oral Legends vs *Written History*

"For us, stories are the wisdom of the people. We learn values from them and from the traditional way of life with its world view. Some tell me this outlook comes from a long-outlived past, but I consider that stories – Udege folklore – are our historical memory and we must not forget them. Most important are the spiritual values. With stories we see how to bring up the younger generation, training them not only to have endurance and strength, but to respect their elders, help the infirm, do no harm to nature, and live in harmony."
NADEZHDA KIMONKO, 2018

In the fall of 2018, I sent an email to Nadezhda Kimonko and her aunt Valentina Kyalundzyuga saying I'd like to come and visit them. They were surprised, since we'd been out of contact for a long time, but the answer was welcoming. Since Nadezhda is the one on the Internet, she and I were in contact over the coming months. When would be a good time? I asked. Not too hot and not too cold? We settled on late April and early May. In the interim, apart from practicalities, we talked about storytelling events.

In spring of 2019, Nadia was waiting at the airport. She seemed shorter than I remembered, probably because she is truly a large person in spirit. Suitcases caused the usual chaos, but things seemed different as soon as we went outdoors. In earlier years, we used a city bus, but this time she took me to a car. It was driven by Alexander Frolenok, who would turn out to be a wonderful helper in every way. In the village, he chopped wood, took beautiful photos, and recorded speakers and singers. He drove tirelessly, laughed easily, and has a deep interest and respect for Indigenous culture. Alexander is Russian, not an Udege, which is one reason that I'm so impressed. Many Russians used to be very insulting about Indigenous people in my experience of the 1990s.

Nadia had laid out a brilliant plan for our activities. In Khabarovsk, we saw everything – from a zoo to some magnificent new churches. The zoo had exotic large birds and animals we rarely see, from a Russian elk to a tiger. In North America, the Russian elk is called a moose, and the animal called elk there is different.

I have never seen a Siberian or Amur tiger, although I often wonder if a tiger had ever watched me when I was walking by the woods near the village. If I ever do see one, my feelings will be mixed – both excitement and fear. It was sad to see that glorious, sacred animal behind a high metal fence, lying sadly it seemed, finally disappearing behind a large rock. There are only about 560 tigers in Russia, and while that is more than there had been five years before, it's not many. We took no photographs.

In the city, we saw a show honouring an Udege jazz singer, and we went to the Khabarovsk Territorial Museum named after N.I. Grodekov, which I always insist on visiting. The Amur River passes by a lovely park, and Nadia says the river is amazingly cleaner than in years before. People can now eat fish from it, which was not possible twenty years ago. Then, people claimed that they had caught a fish with two heads.

I always throw a small pebble from a Vancouver beach into the Amur as a greeting.

After our trips through the villages, we had dinner at Nadia's apartment. It is much larger and more comfortable than the old one, for which she had waited many years. It was not possible to buy apartments and houses in those days, and she had waited years to get a government one. Now, for the first time, they have their own apartment, with enough room. She lives there with her husband and their son, who had been a difficult five-year-old when I last saw him, but was now a polite student of nineteen.

There was also a military parade in Khabarovsk toward the end of my trip. It was difficult for me to watch, since it reminded me of the ones that had terrified me years before. Tanks and huge trucks blocked a street that seemed endless. In past years, the tanks were in a wide, empty square, which is now covered with trees and fountains. Now the parade goes along the streets instead. When asked, Nadia said that people still enjoy having the parade, because it makes them feel they are taken care of by the military. I now understood that many Canadians have never lived through an attack, whereas in Russia many of the elder generation have. The parade was just a practice for the military. It would be Victory Day, marking the surrender of Nazi Germany in 1945. May 2 was the exact day that I had arranged to fly home.

The months before my trip had been full of emails – some practical, but others full of deeper thoughts and questions. I started watching Facebook, which they use much more than I do. There I could see many articles by our friend Lyubov Passar, a number of them about ancient stone figures and more about the national park around Krasny Yar village to the south of Khabarovsk. I looked it up. Bikin National Park consists of 11,604.69 square kilometres, compared with the well-known Banff Park in Canada with 6,641 square kilometres. On the other hand, Wood Buffalo National Park in the north of Alberta, with 44,807 square kilometres, is the largest in Canada.

Nadia told me that some people find that park a great benefit, and others a major problem. Feelings were still mixed, even though the park had been there for several years. I was eager to go there, and even more to see old friends in Gvasyugi.[1]

From Grandmother at the Fire to a Soviet Education and Work

Nadezhda Efimovna Kimonko was born on 6 January 1963, in the small village of Gvasyugi. Her elementary schooling was there, and when it was time for high school, she was taken to a residential school, where she did very well. She recalls excellent teachers, which was very similar to the experience of her aunt Valentina Tunsianovna. When I asked, Nadia did not recall any physical or emotional abuse from teachers, so unlike the experiences of many Indigenous students in Canada.[2]

From that school, Nadezhda went to the Leningrad State Pedagogical Institute. I'm impressed by the high levels of education so many people have there. All this schooling was in the Russian language. In those days, the students were forbidden to speak their native language in school, although they did speak it at home. However, Nadia was fascinated with a wide range of learning, largely about European cultures, and enjoyed the institute entirely, even though it was about 8,700 kilometres away by train. Nevertheless, she was glad to get home afterward.

Nadezhda's family included three other children. Their parents had died early, and she remembers being brought up by her grandmother Kyandu Zandievna and grandfather Yengili Batovich Kimonko before leaving the village. Her early life included long periods out in nature, learning an understanding of animals and plants.

In the evenings, her grandmother told the children *nimanku* – stories from dreams. The following story has various versions, depending on the teller, and this one made the children laugh.

The Story of the Crow. Told by Kyandu Zandievna Kimonko between the Years 1960 and 1980

Many stories like this one were written down the first time by Valentina in her notebook, which was later lost in a fire. Fortunately, a book from 1998 was available outside her home, and I was able to find a version in New York later.

As she was working, many storytellers were dying, and others did not continue. This explains why it's not remembered exactly which year each story was told.

There lived one crow. He lived and lived and then thought, "Hey hey hey … why am I living? I'm going to go away, along my own way." He set off shaking his head, down the river to the sea. He just flew and flew and then he came to the home of old man Kanda. Crow dropped the blanket of the youngest daughter on to the ground and, just like that, hid himself under it.

A little later the elder sister came out of the house and saw that her little sister's blanket had fallen. She went back in and called her sister.

"Little sister, your blanket fell. Go and get it!"

The youngest sister went out, and it was true that her blanket had fallen. She took it down and began to shake it out. Suddenly, out of the blanket fell Crow. The youngest sister put him into the blanket and took it home.

At night, going to sleep, she lay Crow down with her. And that's how Crow started to live.

Then old man Kanda found out that his youngest daughter was living with a crow.

"Well, well, the most loved daughter, whom I so cherished, is living with a crow! Listen, you will not live in my house!"

Old man Kanda took his daughter, and at a distance built her a house made of grass. His daughter started to live alone with her crow. She took all her things, with special attention to her handiwork and her sewing case.

At that time, the eldest sisters were getting married. The sisters and their parents fed their little sister only with things that were being thrown away.

And so, one evening, the youngest daughter went to visit her eldest sisters. They said, "Hey, Belye, tell your husband-crow that all of us are going tomorrow to hunt wild boar."

Belye was angry and went home.

"Hey Crow!" she said. "If you were like a man, you'd also go hunting wild boar tomorrow!"

She flung her Crow onto the blanket and lay down to sleep.

The next day at sunrise, the husbands of the elder sisters went to drive boar. They called Crow, who didn't reply. Laughing, they hurried away on their skis. But Crow slept, hanging his head. It was already midday when he got up. After he awoke, he went, rocking his head, to the road where people carried firewood.

He went further, and called, "Grandmother Bua! Don't forget. Earlier I was Yegdiga! A man!"

Grandmother Bua is known as the whole world.

He hit his own head with a stick, and after that became a strong Yegdiga – a hero. Then he turned back to Grandmother Bua.

"Throw me a horse! A horse with a wagon!

No sooner had he called, when a horse and wagon fell before him. As soon as Yegdiga sat on it, the horse rose upward and flew.

He flew and flew and came down where the others were hunting. Yegdiga said to his horse, "Horse, make dirt on the hunters."

And the horse started to shit. The hunters were surprised.

"What the heck? How strange. Why did that foul hail come in autumn like this instead of the winter?"

Yegdiga flew further. He flew and flew, and then saw wild boars coming. He killed all the boars in a moment. He made copies of boars from their excrement, one by one. He set those back along the road, so that the hunters would see them. He put oil on himself and flew up in his wagon.

He flew and saw that the hunters were coming. Yegdiga said again, "Horse, wet the hunters on the head!"

The horse started to urinate. All those who were below were surprised.

"There's something strange! It's raining in these places – can it be?"

And Yegdiga flew home.

He returned to the *taiga* and came down on the road at a place where people brought firewood. He put the real meat down in the wagon and set off back into the sky. He hid the meat in a hole in a tree. Then he turned back into Crow and set out for home.

In the evening, Belye went to her parents. She arrived and saw that her father and sisters were still eating meat – celebrating! And they never gave her anything.

Her father called, "Mother, Mother! May a crow's wife take boar legs with her?!"

Arriving home, Belye was in a foul mood, and she flung the boar legs on her crow blanket. She lay down to sleep immediately.

She slept and slept, woke up, looked, and saw that it was clear daylight in the house. She thought, "How can I have slept while such light came?!" She went outside and then suddenly she fell as she stepped. Now she understood that it was still night. She looked back into the house and realized that the house was all made of shining gold.

She went in. And yes, the house was all golden. Her old hay house was no longer. Belye was very surprised. She looked, and beside her was a strong Yegdiga – sleeping. And beside him was Crow. She quietly approached, took the crow's *obolochku*, the skin left after changing form. Right away she put it in her sewing basket. She hid it and lay down again.[3]

She wanted to sleep, but couldn't. She got up. She went to Yegdiga and embraced him. And suddenly she was flying onto the floor. Yegdiga had kicked her, but by doing it he saved her life, since something was falling. Belye, the little dove, stood up.

He asked her, "Doesn't it hurt?"

"It's nothing! It's not painful," she replied.

"Where did you put my Crow?" He was angry because she had taken it away.

"Why do you live like that? How can I live with a crow? If you are a man, be a man!" She was angry.

He replied, "Belye, my dear! Bring your father and mother here. We'll give them a meal. They deserve it, the way they have treated you."

"Yesterday in the evening I brought what mother gave me. Shall I feed them nothing but boar legs when they come, or what?" she asked.

"They ate excrement," he said. "It came from boars. Throw all these boar legs away! Tomorrow I will go for real boar meat, which I got myself and put away."

In the morning, Belye prepared her beautiful clothing and every kind of food. But before she called her father and mother, she put on her worst clothing and made her hair messy. She put on her old skin dress made from salmon skin.

Then she went to them.

"Father, Mother, Sisters! Come to me! I sent my Crow for a dead rabbit so that I could feed you."

And then she went back, laughing.

The parents set off, and suddenly saw a very beautiful golden house, which was all shining. When the sisters saw it, they immediately went back home. The father and mother kept going.

But Belye and Yegdiga waited and waited – and no one arrived.

Belye sent Yegdiga, saying, "Go and find out why they are not coming."

They went out and saw that her mother and father wanted to come up to the house, but they couldn't get there. Their lips and face were all scratched and torn – they kept sliding down and falling.

Belye called, "Bring them!"

"And why did the others not come?" asked Yegdiga.

"They ran away out of shame," said the father and mother.

Then they began to celebrate. Father and mother were happy. They spent the night with their daughter.

But in the night, while they were sleeping, their daughter Belye laid *kasha* in their pants. They felt it in their dreams.

The father said, "Mother, Mother, I have fouled myself."

"Father, oh Father, I too have dirtied my pants," she replied.

And, without saying a word, they went home.

When they had gone, Yegdiga said to Belye, "Why did you humiliate your father and mother?"

"I suffered much. They needed to be mocked. And what I did to them was nothing," said Belye.

Father and mother went home and amused themselves. Yegdiga and Belye were married, and they lived well. ▾

How People Moved from the Sea to the Mountains

Sitting with her grandparents, Nadezhda enjoyed humour, and also learned much about her family's history. It was her grandfather Yengili Batovich Kimonko who told her how the Kimonko clan came to live by the inland Khor River long ago. They had lived on the shore of the sea before that – and they were many. Not for nothing, grandfather added, were the Udege called *namunka*, which means "the sea people."

Later Jansi Batovich Kimonko published the first Udege book. This honoured author lived from 1909 to 1949. He wrote that the Kimonko clan took their name from the river Kimo. Now that same river is called Kema, and is located in the Terneiski region, on the waters of Primorsky Territory. His book was entitled *Where the Sukpai Rushes Away*. It showed how people lived in those places, happily under communism.

Under Soviet power, it was very important for all books to include the best of communism. He did his best, but also went into the forest to hide when he thought he might be sent to the camps. The book is still popular, however, especially with people who can see familiar families, places, and work – especially hunting.

Jansi Kimonko also described a tragic flood, when the fish went away in the sea. Days of hunger arrived, and people went into the *taiga*, the Turkic word for forested mountains, as opposed to the cliffs without trees.

When they arrived in Sukpai, they saw many fish in the river and animal tracks on the shore. And so the Kimonko clan stayed to live by the Sukpai River. The river runs below Khabarovsk and above Gvasyugi, and meets the Khor.

Although the people had moved inland, there are many memories of their time by the sea.

The History of a Family. Told by Valentina's Father, Tunsiana Chingisovich Kimonko, to a Relative, Anana Kimonko

One day a boy arrived at the place where people still lived by the sea. They began to use him as a labourer and made him work the bellows. They mocked, teased, and beat him.

And then, one day, when they started to hammer and forge, they began to mock the boy again. He got up and ran, then jumped down from a high precipice. Just before jumping, he told them, "You will die because this land will fall. You'll fall to the bottom and die."

Then he jumped and disappeared. And so, they lost the boy.

From that time on, people started to die there, because the land was falling into the water. They began to run away because of the deaths. People ran inland and found the River Khor – they began to run and then to live there. They came to that place.

The boy had come in his own time to tell the Udege that the land would fall. He came to save them from death. Before that, they all lived on the shore of the sea. There were no islands then, just one large one, but when the earth began to fall, the water rose rose and created smaller ones. From that time on, the Udege began to live inland on the River Khor. ▾

Beginnings of Things, Seen Many Ways

Although we don't know when the story is said to have taken place, Jansi Kimonko told others of his grandfather, who had moved inland following an otter while hunting. He arrived at the Khor River and stayed there.

The time of living on the shore is remembered in several stories, such as one told of a man who fell in love with a seal and went to the underwater world with her. Several other stories taking place on the sea include "The Seagull," about a man who tried to carry women across the water.[4] Indeed, many stories appear about the beginnings of things, people, and places, and the ways they shifted – including the story of Sister and Brother told by Yevdokia Batovna.

Another tale tells how people first came to realize that there was a world under the ground, as well as the ones on earth and in the sky. In the beginning, people were not aware of the places under the ground. Two brothers named Uza and Yegda met up with a large and dangerous animal called Gambau-Buin' and struck him with a spear. A bird then advised the brothers to look at the creature's belly. Inside they found many people who had been eaten, swallowed by Gambau-Buin'. These people spoke to the boys, saying that, without them, they would never have been able to return to this world, and they told the brothers what to do next. Uza dug in the earth and saw the other world: sky, hill, forest, and river. He covered everything with birchbark, which is known to have the ability to open things. Later, Yegda fell down into the underworld, opening it with the birchbark and letting the dead people rest. So it was that *Buhniha*, the underworld, was opened to the dead.

It took me a long time to understand that the two men were both heroes, with Uza's physical strength and Yegda's strong mind. At the end, Yegda was first to open the true way to the place where people belong after death.[5]

Several people write their stories somewhat differently, possibly about different times and places. Some say the question of Udege ancestry is not decided finally, nor is that of other Indigenous peoples in other families' eras. Up until now there have been two points of view. According to the southern view, the Udege came from the southern Manchu. As a result, a stratification of many elements of Paleo-asiatic cultures came to be.

On the other hand, others consider that, because of many elements, both material and spiritual, the Udege and some other people are of northern ancestry. These may be the ones who lived by the sea. Archeological research has established that, in the era of the end of the second thousand years (c. 2000 BC), a tribe came from Siberia, bringing the Tungus language. They arrived in the regions of the lower Amur and northern Primorye.

It is my belief that both are true.

The culture of newcomers mixed with that of the aboriginal population already there, and gradually created one ethnic community. Ancestors of today's Udege and Nanai peoples of Primorye are genetically and culturally connected with the tribes of those regions during the Middle Ages.

The Mongols also played an important role in the history of the Udeges' ancestors. Their actions brought massive moving and mixing among many peoples of the region. It is considered that these ethnic processes became the basis for the formation of the Manchu, Nanai, Udege, Oroch, and other people very close to the Udege. Oral stories include fighting amongst Chinese, Japanese, Mongols, and Udege.[6]

I'm always impressed by the oral memories of the Indigenous people, their storytelling, and the ways they can connect with written accounts.

How People Moved Inland from the Shore. Told by Nikita Nyambuevich Kyalundzyuga from the 1960s to the 1980s

The Udege set off to fight, crossing the Khor hill and going further away, together with their troops. On the slope named *Dudekhe*, a small hill, they stopped for a daytime rest before going to fight with the Chinese. During that rest, they made an earthen embankment and put up a mountain, so that they would not be seen while resting. The leaders hid behind the mountain and hid their troops.

In the evening the Udege leader said, "All who lie with their heads pointing backward will stay in place, and all who lie with their heads pointing forward, will go forward.

"Those who don't want to go forward put their heads back."

In the morning those whose heads had lain forward got up and set off on their way. The others stayed sleeping and didn't notice them go. All those who laid with their heads back, stayed where they were, and then they all went back. Each one began to live in a good area by himself.

Those who went to fight, fought with the Chinese. They stayed in the Chinese territory and began to live there with their own leader. The Chinese chased after the Udege, who could not defeat the Chinese. And then they began to run. They found a separate small hill standing, and stopped there for a daytime rest before the battle. As soon as the Chinese came after them, they started fighting with them. The Chinese had two leaders, and the Udege killed one of them. The Chinese ran back.

The Udege fighters returned to their former place, and there they stayed. All who stayed and didn't go to fight with the Chinese, remained to live in the *taiga*, where we know them now.

At first the Udege came from the sea, crossed the Khor, and crossed many hills. All the time fighting, they went into China with their own troops. All who stayed went different ways, each on his own. Wherever they wanted, they became the forest Udege. ▾

It is hard to understand today that a certain narrow area is part of Russia – west and east, between China and the sea. At one point, north and south between Khabarovsk and Vladivostok, there were Chinese and Japanese people. The Chinese had come from a corner of Manchuria where there are fewer people even now. There were Japanese too, who had come over the water.

And so it is that, for many years, the Udege lived nomadically in the forests, while still wearing beautiful embroidery and eating from elaborate wooden plates with delicate ornaments of animals and flowers. They were all made by hand with a knife, the way they had at a time when they stayed in one place. They came to live in a village again only under the Soviets in the early 1990s.

There have been many more wars and calm periods in-between.

The next legend may very well go back even farther in time. It must have been told during some of Valentina Tunsianovna's storytelling evenings, which would have been interesting for all. Among other things it brings back the *singmu*, now a mythic crocodile that can appear like a snake. It's a rare one that is kind to children. The next story takes us to different nationalities.

Legend: How the Land Shifted, How Children Were Saved by a Crocodile (*Singmu*), and How the Family became Udege, Korean, Chinese, and Japanese. Told by Igru Gaikalyevich Kyalundzyuga between 1960 and 1980[7]

A man and his wife lived. They had two children, a girl and a boy. Rain poured and poured without stopping, and all the time the children played together. Once they played and played, walking along a path where they carried their firewood. They walked further and further, and then saw a *bal-*

agan, a house where people carried out the offering for *Bua* – prayer.[8] They looked inside and there, drawn on paper, was the image of leader wolves and red helper wolves. The children looked and then they went home, saying nothing to their father or mother. Day after day they played and completely forgot that they had seen a sacred little house.

Then one day they remembered and went there to look again. From the sacred hut came a grey-grey old man.

"Why have you come here," he asked.

The children replied, "We came to look at the house."

The grey-grey old man said, "Children, come here any time, come but don't tell anyone. The earth must turn over, everything is changing. When the leader of wolves and the leader of red wolves let sparks come from their mouths, don't be afraid. Go straight along the path in the *taiga*. Along the road you'll see a lake, and in it there will be a *singmu*. Bow to him seven times, and the snake himself will explain."

Did the children know that the *singmu* was a huge and frightening crocodile, who usually wants to eat a human immediately on sight? We don't know.

The children started to walk as the old man had told them. Every day they walked and played around the big tent.

Once they came. Sparks were coming from the mouth of the leader wolves and red helper wolves. The girl and her younger brother went out of the *balagan* and set off along the path into the *taiga*. They walked and walked and saw a lake. There was the crocodile. The children bowed to the crocodile seven times. When they had bowed seven times, the *singmu* spoke in a human voice.

"Sit on my back. As soon as a strong wind blows and trees begin to fall, get into my mouth. Sit there. When it gets light all around, come back out."

The girl and her younger brother climbed onto the crocodile and started playing there. They played, and at once a strong wind came up. Trees began falling. The children were frightened, and they ran. The girl remembered what the *singmu* had said, and she dove with her brother into the crocodile's mouth. They looked around – and inside there was a house. Oh! what kinds of delicious food were there!

Many many days passed – they forgot how many. And then all was light around them, and they came back out of doors. What bright light there was! It made their eyes hurt to look. They looked around well and saw that their house now stood on a tiny island. On the island there was a little low hill, and, beyond that, everything was water. Wherever you looked there, everything was water.

There they lived, and that way they grew up.

The elder sister said, "Hey, my brother, shall we go ahead and get married?"

"It would not be good," said the younger brother. "How can a brother and sister marry?"

The grey-grey old man appeared and spoke very suddenly, "You want to marry?"

The sister said, "Yes! Let's get married!"

The old man pointed. "You see that corn mill built of stones on top of each other? Elder sister, you take the round one that is below, and younger brother take the other one, above. Lift them up to the top of the hill and then let them go down, each taking its own direction. These round stones will roll down the hill. Let them go whichever way they want to roll. And you, each one of you, go in your own direction. If these stones come together in one place again, then you will become wife and husband."

So he spoke, and immediately disappeared again.

The sister took the lower round stone and the brother the upper round stone and they went up the hill. They came to the top of the hill and let the stones go down, each in its own direction. The sister and brother each followed one stone. They ran, ran, and just then, at the bottom of the hill, the two round stones came together, and sister and brother met near the stones.

Right away they married. In time they gave birth to children, and later each of the children married. They had so many children that there was very little room on the island.

A bird flew by there. She flew seven days and seven nights without rest. She was tired of living in one place, all the time above the water and swimming on the water, and so she flew, not sitting on the water.

She flew and flew and then saw an old woman, who stood, one foot on a tiny island. The bird asked for *blage* – spiritual good fortune.

"Babushka, allow me to sit on your land!"

The old woman did not allow her. She didn't allow her at first, but finally agreed. A little move gave her just enough room so that the bird could sit.

After some time, the old woman began to drive the bird away. She was tired of fussing with this little bit of land anyway. Now the bird, in flight, caught soil with her claws where they stood.

The bird continued to fly and fly, and the earth from her claws all fell and fell. And where the earth fell, a large piece of land grew at the same time. So she flew and let them fall.

The children went to live on these growing lands, each with a wife or husband. All of those who moved there began to call themselves by different names: some Udege, some Chinese, some Korean, and others Japanese. In this way, they grew up, each on his own land, all with children born from one father and one mother.[9] ▼

City Life and Dance

Nadezhda Efimovna did not live in the villages for any great time after childhood, and when she finished university, she felt that her calling was in the city. Once she told me that most Udege cannot tolerate city life, and since she is able, she needs to stay. She works with young people there teaching song and dance and choreography and arranging performances. "Culture must stay alive for the youth," she says.

After graduation, she moved to the coastal east for a while and taught history to the early grades in schools in the coastal Primorsky Territory, to the southeast, a long way from her own home in Gvasyugi. That seacoast can be reached only by water, and boats came rarely.

After that she moved to Khabarovsk, and she has worked with education since 1990, promoting the culture of her young people.

She has had a long history leading dance ensembles and singers, plus writing books and guiding foreigners. She is an excellent organizer and coordinator, leading cultural activities, including festivals in regions on the territorial level and beyond. Remembering her grandmother's ancient stories and songs, she has worked with other guardians of folklore. This explains how she so easily found many elder storytellers when we travelled to hear stories during my first years there – at least twenty-two in two weeks in 1993.

Nadezhda Efimovna has been repeatedly honoured by the Ministry of Culture of Khabarovsk Territory and the Russian Federation for her fruitful work and active part in the cultural life of the territory and the far-eastern region. Her official job has a long title: Director of the Department of Traditional Culture – the House of People's Creativity of the Territory of Khabarovsk and Educational Association of Creative Culture.

She recalls being forbidden to speak her native language in high school. "This was not so long ago," she points out, and others agree.

"Now they teach the Udege language in schools," she says. "Although the way it's spoken is different than at home. Children don't speak it now as we did when we were young."

I learned a little of the language, but she knows I wouldn't understand the more colloquial language, and so uses it only with others, often for humour.

In a different generation, some parents have grown up speaking Russian, without the native language. They passed Russian to their children, since it is the only official language of this huge country – with the exception of a few, such as Sakha, in Yakutia. There is still work to be done with language and stories, but it seems clear that Nadezhda and Valentina's children will take up an ancestral language with the help of their parents.

Indigenous people in most of Russia receive a notably good education, and are lucky that for many years there have been teachers among their own people. Recently, they have also been bringing their own languages back to schools, often by using stories. Others have noted that treatment in the boarding schools in Russia has varied quite a lot.

On the other hand, I think of the appalling residential schools of Canada during the same time that many of the schools were opened in Russia. In Canada, the Truth and Reconciliation Commission of 2008 to 2015 pointed out that four thousand children had died, and those who lived suffered terrible treatment – including the sexual abuse of at least seven thousand children. The numbers were most likely significantly greater. This is known in my country as cultural genocide. We suffer from shame and the need for action.

Russia seems to have done much better in these schools, although there has certainly been a lot of public racism – at least in the early nineties. On my earlier trips, I saw it frequently on buses or in other public places. People would push aside from an Udege woman very obviously, sneering at her until she cried when she got home. I heard that fights outside schools were common, but in the present I saw friends and co-workers showing very open respect and friendship, with warm conversation and laughter. Still, racism doesn't disappear that fast and does still exist in the lives of Indigenous people.

Storytelling Events

As a result of Nadezhda Kimonko's current work, her groups not only give large dance performances but also organize contests bringing storytelling to the public. I saw one of these storytelling events on my computer before my trip. There were twenty storytellers taking part, some boys and girls as young as seven and adults up to seventy or more. Most were wearing colourful Udege embroidery and backgrounds on their clothes – red, yellow, blue, green, white. You can see it here![10]

Most of the tellers told their stories bilingually, and these ran up to fifteen minutes in length. All of them were traditional stories. Most jury members are teachers, and they judge with attention to "rule and tradition." I'm assuming that "rule" means correct grammar and "tradition" helps children to learn the ancestral language using words that don't have simple meanings in modern thought. One example is the Crow's *obolochku*, meaning the skin left after the bird magically changes from crow to man in the Crow story. "Tradition" could also include good behaviour, understanding singing, ceremony, style, intonation, and rhythm.

Parents, grandparents, and children may still be telling stories at home, although television often takes over, as it does in much of the world. A generation has forgotten storytelling, with the exception of Valentina Tunsianovna and her daughters. The contests bring storytelling back to a new generation – in person.

Other story events include the presentation of theatrical versions of a tale, with more than one actor. Valentina Tunsianovna may also introduce songs, teaching certain musical parts of stories that are important. Tellers may also sing, either to represent shamans or for simple pleasure.

Clearly the Internet is valued in both kinds of education, both language and style.

Nadezhda Efimovna goes on to say, "In the Nanai village of Jari we put on our first storytelling contest in 2014. One chair of the jury was the teacher of the Nanai language at the school, Antonia Sergeevna Kilye. Another member of the jury was Valentina Kyalundzyuga. The two carried out master classes and taught how to tell stories, always by rule and by tradition, with special attention to intonation and rhythm. These are a must, and not just something added on." These things are vital if the people are to keep their culture together.

How lucky the young people are to learn from Valentina Tunsianovna and Nadezhda Efimovna, and even to wear the embroidered clothing of their ancestors. They see a larger picture than just words on paper. I had a similar benefit in the 1990s when an earlier group of elders was still alive and we sat together, with them telling their stories instead of reading them. Most of their stories were told in two languages – one was a kind of music for me, since my understanding of the Udege language is minimal. I was able to just follow a story, since they are so familiar. Of course, most of us now are telling stories in very different settings than the elders did, and stories change, as they have through the years.

Nadia continues with something different. "In the village of Gvasyugi, there was no such contest as the one you've seen. But for two years, they gathered to chat in their native language and they organized contests of language rather than stories.

"In Gvasyugi the language is still taught only in the lower grades. Last year Valentina Tunsianovna put together an Udege language book for Grade 2, and soon she will have one for Grade 3, printed in St Petersburg. Much time goes into this work. Although I don't have those books, I do have two others. She keeps working and more will come from the Khabarovsk book publisher.

"Meanwhile Olesia Vladimirovna Shamshur, a granddaughter of Valentina Tunsianovna, conducted the presentation of a new storybook and told stories to the residents of Gvasyugi. The ensemble Su Gagpai, prepared a theatrical version of the story 'Two Suns,' with storyteller Valentina Tunsianovna in the role of the main hero."

Canada

In Canada in 2019 there were storytelling contests, usually in restaurants, using very short personal stories, and the storytellers were unpaid. Professional tellers went into schools and found work at festivals and other events on their own, sharing tales in a non-competitive setting. For years we also met once a month to share stories. They usually took about twenty minutes each, and the tellers often wished they had more time. Tales may be traditional from various nationalities, personal or family tales, jokes, or other humorous stories. This style has been public since the early 1970s, and we hope something similar will continue.

In many cities there has been an annual "Epic Day" or "Epic Weekend," a different epic each year. The epic may come from any nation, generally one represented in our multicultural cities. For a long time, I organized those in Vancouver, usually with about twenty storytellers, each telling a section of the epic. We thoroughly enjoyed the learning and the event itself. In all these events, the tellers may use any style of speaking, sometimes adding song or musical instruments. The variety is fun and can shed new light on the story.

Clearly our intention is different from that of the Udege. The approaches are very different, and yet they both bring stories to the public. However, their aim is to keep their own art alive, and ours is to bring various cultures together. Both are extremely valuable.

Now I see even more clearly that my friends in Russia have important goals that are different from ours. Dual languages, keeping their own culture alive, learning the music as well as the words and intonation all give an important depth to a given story. The difference from most Canadian storytelling is that the Russian tellers have strict teachers, while for the most part we have a lot of variety – which is inevitable in Canada, since we have storytellers from many countries. The result is that we showcase very different voices and approaches, from China, India, Iran, South Africa, and many others.

Some aspects of the storytelling events held in Cuba, and in Romania, and in other formerly communist countries, have retained competitive characteristics that have been common not only in sports, but also in the arts. I'm not sure if they ever include bilingualism, as the Udege do. Some other festivals I've heard about have provided translators for foreigners. The difference between Cubans and Canadians is often that the former communists tell their story using their teacher's style.

I still feel that being critical in a storytelling contest is questionable, but that's just my opinion. The Udege children get help in improving their skills and enjoy ancient tales. On the other hand, we Canadians have a great variety of styles in performers to enjoy.

One thing is certain. It's no surprise that more artistic activity may go on in Gvasyugi than other villages, since Valentina Tunsianovna is behind them. They have their own events, including one where she invites the villagers to traditional ceremonies, encouraging them to keep the traditions alive.

Here is a story that might be used in a contest. The length is right. On the other hand, it would require some explanation for many children and adults. The *singmu* here is not the helpful one we saw in the previous story, but instead is dangerous to a boy who was not careful enough.

The story will lead us into a fascinating book by Nadezhda Efimovna Kimonko and Valentina Tunsianovna Kyalundzyuga about places, their names and meaning.

Another *Singmu* Story That Didn't End as Well. Told by Irgu Gaikalyevich Kyalundzyuga, Who Lived from 1911 to 1974. The Story Was Told between 1960 and 1974

He also told Lugi Belye's story to Valentina Tunsianovna for us. Here it is:

High at the mouth of the channel Soli, running into the Khor River, there lived a *singmu*. A man came on his boat from the Nanai lands to strip off birchbark. He went across mountains in the direction of Soli, and came to *Mari Binku*, meaning "the place where people lived before." His son was with him. On his back he had a carrier pot made of iron. Along the way he fell on a stone and broke the pot. That place was called *Ene Bayarku*, which means "that crossing."

Here, beside a lake, there were many birch trees. The man stripped and stripped them. His son called him.

"Father, I want to drink. I'll go to the water." He walked to the lake, but unfortunately, he was seen getting there.

"You must come back! Don't go!" The father called, "You should come back! Don't go!" The father had already stripped many birches. Well, after a while the man went down to the lake. He saw that on the lake lay the *singmu*, a big snake, right on the water. Clearly, he had just killed a boy!

The man brought all the birches over to the shore of the lake on his carrier. Setting them on fire, he began to throw them into the water to the *singmu* – who gobbled them all. The man threw and threw the birches. The *singmu* began to eat, and then swam to the surface. The birches began to burn, and the belly of the *singmu* was full of fire. He came to the surface, burned, and began to die. The man took the spear, dragged it with a hook, and opened the *singmu's* belly. He didn't find his son, but managed to find only one little finger.

The Nanai man killed the *singmu* that had four horns, and after that no one heard of him again. The lake was hot, and after that no one saw the *singmu*. At the place where the *singmu* lived, the water has always been red.

Some have called the *singmu* a dragon, whereas others say that dragons only live in China and that the *singmu* can be found further north like this one. Who knows, perhaps those are just different languages, and all are now stories? ▼

Master of the Water: Science and Folklore[11]

Many books about Udege culture have been put together by Valentina Kyalundzyuga, most with stories. However, at one point it was necessary for her to have maps made, with the names of the rivers, lakes, and mountains of her area. This got her interested in their names. Then Nadezhda Kimonko joined in, and in 2016 a fascinating book came out, this time illustrated mostly with large and beautiful photographs of people of all ages riding on boats with trees painted on the sides. The text introduces the names of waterways, landscapes, and people, as well as many short stories.

They have named the book *Мир Хозяина Воды Лунгиэ* (*Master of the Water, Lungiye*) to honour the ancient ruler of water. Like so many mythic characters, *Lungiye* can be kind or cruel, making the water calm or rough. People can drown or make their living. He watches over floods and the formation of rivers and islands.

Valentina Tunsianovna explains that people have long believed in spiritual masters of land, water, and air. Besides *Lungiye*, these include *Ganikhe* and the helper *Temu* as keepers of the water, while *Mamasadavan* is mistress of salmon. Most honoured is the master of fire – *Lydya adzani*.

The book combines science along with the experience and folklore of these hunters, fishermen, and story gatherers, whose memories were completely oral. Names have been important for orienting pathfinders – helping them to remember ways in the forest and finding the right way to go and come back. The pathfinders can understand every detail, how to find the best, most practical, places to live. No wonder they are called the "Forest People." They see nature's signs, the height of mountains, the shorelines of the Tatary Strait, *taiga* paths, and complex rivers. Winter snow and tracks show the paths of neighbours, both human and animal.

The book is full of short stories coming from tales told by real people. Here is one of them, #37.

How One River Was Named *Tagemu*, or Clothing. Told by Michina Kimonko[12]

Long ago an Udege family went hunting for bear and got a small bear baby. Grandma Khaida Kyalundzyuga began to feed him together with her dogs. In the fall, the little bear was growing and began to wander in the forest in search of a place for a winter sleep. Finding a hollow, he began to scratch the tree with his claws, leaving marks. Then he returned to Khaida, demanding food. This went on for quite a while, and people didn't understand why he didn't lie down and sleep. So that the little bear would no longer come to the place where people lived, they hung a dress of grandma Khaida's on the bear's chosen tree. Only then would he lie down in his hollow. The little river that the tree grew on was called *Tagemu*. ▾

The people understand river systems and where they all go. I recall the day years ago we had been fishing from a boat along a complex of rivers and creeks. The river went here and there, such that I would never have found my way back, but the young man working the boat had no problem. We stopped for a picnic, and the women suddenly realized we had no salt for the fish and potatoes. Instead of taking the boat a fair distance back to the nearest house, he walked through the forest. I followed him, and it turned out that the house was not far at all. On the way, he showed me where a bear had slept on grassy ground – another thing I wouldn't have noticed.

As the hunters and fishermen moved, they needed ways to keep track of their location. Knowing and remembering oral folk poems, history, and mythology helped them. Rivers, fish, how they flow – people know all this like an open book learned from childhood. Names can show the depth of the water and how fast it runs, and the characteristics of water, landscape, and more. People can also identify where they find themselves working, by using the names of rivers and their tributaries.

Traditional ways, myths, shamanic practices – all are connected with religious beliefs and models of the world. The waterways and their names have symbolic meanings. Valentina Tunsianovna and Nadezhda Efimovna explain that the name of the river Dakpa means "to disturb or harm." According to the storyteller Yengili Kimonko, when people hunted on that river there were always problems, and the hunt was unsuccessful. Udege who believe in spirits say that they can disturb the hunt and life. This is why they called the river Dakpa. To get rid of that unclean power, they made a doll from straw, in the shape of a person, skewered it on a stick for stability, and then conducted a ceremony. A shaman instilled the bad spirit into the straw figure, and then the shaman's helper took it out and threw it in the direction of the sun.

In the practice of the people there are widely used geographic terms that are connected with local flora and fauna, with picking berries, as well as with preparing firewood and birchbark. The names of several Udege waterways align with titles of clans or tribes. Some place names keep ancient national names alive.

The story here is connected with place names that carry traditional images of life – a junction of history, time periods, and the geography of a country, territory, region, city, or village. At the same time, people remembered details of land, plants, birds, and all the external world.

Valentina Tunsianovna and Nadezhda Efimovna found all the connections between the people and waterways as they reveal the character of lives and cultures. Always showing the meanings of the names and where they are from, they analyzed 160 river names. For example, one tributary of the Khor is *Kadadi*, or *Kada*, meaning a stone. It means stone and mud, reflecting the character of a river full of large boulders.

Another Courageous Woman Hunter. Told by the Hunter Tsambuli Kyalundzyuga

There is a river named *Akhbio-Khualikchi*, or "Kill the Elk."

The brave woman hunter Yapchi Kimonko went hunting every winter in the place of her husband, Tunsiana Kimonko. Once, when she went hunting alone, she saw the fresh tracks of an elk on the snow and began to track him – all day. Yapchi did not have a gun, and so she tied her knife on a long pole. The elk, angry and evil, began to attack, and the brave hunter thrust her knife into him. The animal jumped in all directions against the onslaught of the small woman, until he got tired. Using the moment, the brave woman hunter put her knife in deeper. She was very small, Yapchi, and brave, the first of the hunters, woman or man, who killed an elk with only a knife. After that her relatives were proud of her and named the river in memory of this story.[13] ▼

4

LYUBOV VLADIMIROVNA PASSAR

The Doctor's Clinic and Politics, with Honour to the Tiger. Summer 2019

"I was born in Krasny Yar, known as the capitol of the Udege," said Lyubov Passar. "But all my life I have lived in Khabarovsk. What joy it is to be home now! Luxurious nature with a clean river, a riot of greenery, and the air, sated with the colour of lime – you can drink it like honey! And now, a new hospital with modern equipment and a new apartment provided to me – what else is needed to work with pleasure?!!!

"And to honour the sacred Tiger! My people, the Udege, always revered the tiger as a symbol of the Highest Power. We have respected the tiger, feared and protected him, and killing a tiger was always taboo. They are still around us.

LYUBOV PASSAR, 2019

Earlier Friendship – Shamanism and a Doctor

My first meeting with Lyubov Passar was in Khabarovsk around 1993. She was living there at the time, and was working as a medical doctor and psychiatrist, primarily treating alcoholism. She also felt called as a shaman and was allowing some of those shamanic feelings to be part of her ordinary medical work.[1]

Years later, in 2005, people saw on television that a new shaman was emerging in the village of Krasny Yar: Vasili Dunkai. Valentina Tunsianovna, Lyubov, and I found a ride to go there and meet him. I didn't realize until we were on the way that Krasny Yar was Lyuba's childhood home before she moved to Khabarovsk. We had a wonderful time picnicking on the road, with big trees cooling the heat, and then enjoying a field full of glorious golden lilies as we watched the forest ebb. Later, the new shaman took us out in his boat, and we swam in the river. An old friend of Valentina Tunsianovna's, Alexander Kanchuga, put the two of us up overnight, while Lyubov went to friends of her own. I did not hear anything about the National Park in Krasny Yar that year, since it was just opening.

In 2019, I saw Lyuba once again. Professionally, she was, and still is, busy with medicine as well as politics, both local and global. This includes a spiritual connection with tigers and their lives and health. She had just received a new job in Krasny Yar. "I am really very grateful to the National Park Bikin," she wrote just before I arrived, "and for those transformations that have occurred in my native Krasny Yar – the building of the bakery and a place called the 'House of Daily Life' going up near the hospital; the construction of a new building, where offices of the administration and precinct inspector are in place; as well as an apartment for the police officer. Stable electricity and high-speed Internet are about to come. The head of the village has very big plans for the improvement of the village, receiving the support of the regional authorities. My native village has the highest potential for development! And so I will return to my birthplace to work as a doctor in the local clinic."

By the time of my visit in 2019, I had read about the Bikin National Park. It had become first a major issue and later a calming down, as Lyuba says – with benefits. I soon came to find that the word *Bikin* can refer to the park, and to a fairly large town, a river, titles, and even the purse I bought before leaving Krasny Yar.

Everyone told me about the park and, little by little, I learned. There were forty Amur tigers in the park at one recent count. Beyond that, 35 per cent of the salmon come from the Russian Far East, along with other fish.[2]

From the city we went through one village to another, from Gvasyugi to Krasny Yar, from there back to the city, finally going north to see friends there. We chatted as we bumped over long dirt roads, and later over better ones. One day, Nadia told me about Pavel Sulyandziga, a man I had not met and who now lives in the United States. He had been the first to organize the national park. As Nadia told me more, I realized I would certainly want to find him when I got home.

The Russian Amazon

Pavel Sulyandziga says that the *taiga* in the Bikin River Valley has become a pilgrimage site for scientists studying biodiversity and climate change. First, this taiga is considered to be the largest preserved forest in the northern hemisphere, and it produces the largest amount of oxygen. It is called the Russian Amazon.

"Because the taiga in the Bikin River valley is the place where north and south meet, it is home to native plants and animals from both directions. Larch, cranberries, and other northern plants grow next to southern plants such as wild grapes and lotus. It is interesting to observe how 'the north' and 'the south' have converged in this one place.

"Others agree that our greatest treasure is the Amur tiger, the largest cat on earth and an ancestor of the Udege.

"There are also huge reserves of gold on our territory and massive coal deposits," he says. "They're the third largest by volume in the Far East. There is also a large volume of wood, especially valuable species such as cedar, oak, pine, and ash. To preserve our environment, we entered into the Kyoto Protocol and took part in its emissions-trading market.

"There are also 194 species of birds. Nine of them are in the Red Book of Russia – a state record established for documenting rare and endangered species of animals, plants, and fungi. UNESCO lists the upper Bikin area as one of the Global Nature Legacies."[3]

Nadia said, "He is the leader of the Udege, and beside that, he's a poet."

Pavel Sulyandziga – Dedicated Leader, Activist, and Artist[4]

An Udege man has two forces in life –
These two help him to live.
Love of his native country and family –
The threads of generations.

They soar surely on the heights
As if on wings of a proud bird,
Allowing themselves a striving toward heaven,
They see the earth in all its beauty.
They help when suddenly bad weather

Makes the soul stray along the way,
Then come together – the Udege has joy,
Flying, while their ancestors
Are *mafa-kuti* – the Tiger.

Here on a foreign land, much is near by,
All gives joy to the eye, and the family is with me.
Children are happy – for them everything is superb.
Still, I find no place for myself.
Vandals have taken away my native land,
Those with no friends know nothing of kinship.
... and I fly like a bird, far away
Missing one of my wings.

PAVEL SULYANDZIGA

Dr Pavel Sulyandziga is well known as the Udege's long-time leader. He was born in Krasny Yar, although he now lives in the United States. When I sent a message to him after my trip, I felt shy, since I hadn't met him in person, and he is well known from Krasny Yar to the United Nations in New York. At this point he lives in Maine, on the northeast coast.

He replied right away. "Of course I'll help in your project. I'm very glad you have been to my home village and met my people." Sure enough, yet another extraordinarily hospitable Udege.

Since then, we have had many conversations. He is learning English, and I am improving my Russian writing. I heard all about the family, the children who were growing up and the parents proud of their success at school. And they were singing – even in Carnegie Hall. More recently, two of them were winners in the "President's Education Award Program." Of course, they learned the language a lot faster than their parents. As the poem says, it is superb for them and painful for him. His wife is also working hard.

Why did they move to Maine? The time came that Pavel's life was threatened in Krasny Yar, and the family had to leave Russia very fast. "That was why we came here," Pavel says. "We needed to leave immediately, and we did not know where to go. A woman from home had married an American man and come to the United States. They invited us and helped us get set up. We even lived in their home in the beginning, and met their friends."

Pavel had received death threats in response to his activities to protect the rights of Indigenous peoples in Russia. I have hesitated to ask more about that, wondering whether the threats had come from the government or from local people who did not like the idea of the national park. Some members of the group that favoured the national park have lost their jobs, and one has even seen his property destroyed. Still, they all persevere.

Nadezhda Kimonko told me that Pavel Sulyandziga is the much-honoured leader of the Udege people and was the key player in bringing the Bikin National Park to life.

Although by now he is busy with valuable work in the United States, he hopes that one day he and his family may return to their homeland. On the other hand, the children are now at home with their school and friends.

Most recently he and his brother Rodion Sulyandziga, who is still living in Russia, have put together a group called "Bikin and Udege" in Vladivostok. It is to publicize everything that has to do with the Bikin and the Udege people. It includes the forest, its history and news. Some people are working with bringing back the Udege language, and can be found on Facebook at *Бикин и Удэге* (Bikin and Udege).

The Udege and Nanai people make up most of the population in Krasny Yar, and many still carry on their traditional way of life, including hunting, fishing, and gathering plants. They are continuing to care for nature with methods used by their ancestors. People wish to preserve all of this.

In 2013, Putin's government decided that conservation of the Amur tiger and leopard populations was a priority. For that reason, they decided to set up a national park in the Bikin basin, and included Indigenous people in the management. The government of the Russian federation now helps to keep up the park, although many local people object to its presence and feel that it takes away local power.

At first, my friend Lyubov seemed to be very much against having a national park in Krasny Yar, citing other places where the government had failed to honour its promises. She repeated her words several times. "During the creation of national parks in places of traditional residence of Indigenous peoples, the original idea has been turned into a complete travesty. That's the problem."

Later, she appeared to be in favour, since a park could stop many of the poachers that came in from China and other places. She came to agree with Pavel Sulyandziga, one of the first to organize the national park. Other people remained unsatisfied with the plan, realizing that some of the park's land can be rented out to citizens and businesses for recreational activities. This they knew would damage their livelihood, which continues to be hunting.

Who is still against the park now? The woodworker Vladimir Sulyandziga in Krasny Yar spoke about it when Alex and I were looking at his beautiful artwork. Sulyandziga has lived there all his life.

"We Udege have become different people," he said. "We've damaged nature – a thing our ancestors never did. We took wood only when needed, and now so much is taken."

I thought of how much logging we had seen. Those forests, rich with ash, linden, and cedar, were gradually disappearing.

"It's huge and unending," Vladimir continued. "All of that timber is probably sent to other countries. I'm not sure if it is anything to do with the park. Ginseng is now taken by poachers, and we feel badly – we're not like that. It's all about money now. All Russia is not good."

Problems of Another Park

Nadezhda Kimonko wrote about parks back in 2018, before my trip.

> Some people are against them because a national park means the establishment. The significance of it is in the federal government. A similar park, named "Anyuiskii," is located in the Nanai region of Khabarovsk Territory. It's been there for several years now. There the authorities do not permit the Udege hunters to hunt and fish. I'm afraid that such a situation might also arise in Primorye Territory.
>
> Lyuba Passar is in favour of the creation of a national park in Krasny Yar because many rich poachers are in the *taiga* there. Authorities stand as a "hunting-military," and protect the *taiga* from those poachers. You see, we need to have the park because of the poachers that are there now. There must be a place for the

hunters, so that they can protect the *taiga*, including tigers, from the poachers.

"As for me, I'm not absolutely certain where I am with this situation. It's hard to say whether I'm for or against. It's unknown what will happen. They are putting in a new chief – a boss who is not a local person – so it's possible the same situation may arise as in the *Anyuiskii* park. In the beginning they promised much, but it's not clear what is happening now.

Meanwhile, in the village of Krasny Yar there is positive change: they're building houses, making a bridge, preserving and honouring objects of social-cultural meaning, and they say that there will be electric light twenty-four hours a day. But who knows?

Zapvednik is a reserve, and can be strict about activity. However, I've learned that people were most against the park because they wanted their own land.

I was wondering what objects of "social-cultural meaning" might be. Perhaps the stone I saw in Krasny Yar honouring Dersu Uzala, a skilled guide who helped Vladimir Arsenyev in his explorations? He was later made famous in a movie by the brilliant filmmaker Akira Kurosawa. Or was it the beautiful place for picnics beside the river, or a museum of crafts – embroidery, woodwork, and a tool used for softening skins? It could be that and more.

Nadia went on,

Krasny Yar has always had tourism. I think that they already have more now. A number of people have put together a community called "Tiger," which is very strong, largely dealing with foods. When I hear an opinion from the side of the national park, I understand that they have a powerful lobby.

True, there are some benefits to having the national park. When more people came there, it was inevitable that poachers came too, many of them from the very near parts of China. Lyubov Passar, like most, is glad to have them watched for the whole village. This is an important point.

Beside that, with the national park comes help from WWF, UNESCO, and RAIPON, the Russian Association of Indigenous Peoples of the North. Its purpose is to protect Indigenous peoples'

> human rights, defend their legal interests, assist in solving environmental, social, economic, cultural, and educational issues, and to promote their right to self-governance. RAIPON works with the State Duma and the government of the Russian Federation regarding legislation related to Indigenous peoples' issues.

And now Lyubov has a job as doctor in the new medical clinic and the people have medical aid without making long journeys to find it when herbal medicine is not enough.

Government

Without a doubt there are things to be concerned about in the Russian government. As of 2007, it had abstained from the UN Declaration on the Rights of Indigenous Peoples, and since then, though several countries have changed, Russia has not, as far as I can see.

Newspapers from 2014 said that, in spite of their leader, most people were very much against the park, owing to massive violations of the rights of Indigenous people in different places, the deterioration of their land, plants, nature, and the possibility of losing their hunting. In June 2014, many people in Krasny Yar prepared to have a rally against the park, fearing it would deprive them of access to their ancestral land and their livelihoods.

The park project went through in spite of those who were opposed to it. Between then and now, many people have been satisfied and are happy with the results. A few are still against it.

For generations, Udege women have been bold and intelligent, and continue with politics as well as working as educators and researchers. They are remembered in stories from earlier times. Belye is always a story heroine who has great skills, beauty, and problems to overcome. Lyubov Passar has a lot in common with her.

Here is a story that shows a mix of a patriarchal family with very powerful women. I like this story with the woman who lives on her own, even after her child is born. That part is similar to my own family and upbringing. Valentina frequently mentions stories like this.

Belye. How She Helped a Young Boy and Defeated the Brothers Who Said "We Don't Need You." Told by Valentina Kyalundzyuga, Printed in 1974 and Reprinted in 2018 in the Book *Dva Solntsa* (*Two Suns*)

There lived an old man named Kanda Mafa, and his old woman. Their one and only daughter was named Belye. She grew up beautiful and an artist – she could make designs from birchbark and fish skin. She sewed herself a beautiful robe, a *khalat*, with designs.

Old man Kanda Mafa thought, and then said, "Daughter mine, you are all we have. We are getting old. Who will look after us? We will not give you to anyone in marriage."

Belye said, "Build me a birch house by the sea, so that no one can see me and come to me," said Belye.

Kanda Mafa built a birch *balagan* to be her house. It stood over the sea for their daughter Belye, and she began to live there. Then one night a powerful hurricane came up and carried the birch house away to sea. In the birch house was Belye.

The house was carried a long time on the sea, thrown from one side to the other. It came to the shore where the brothers Biatu lived.

Belye begged them, "Brothers Biatu, take me into your birch house. I will sew clothes, shoes, and gloves. I will cook your food."

The brothers replied, "We don't need you."

Belye went further on the water. She went further and came to a sandy shore. Somehow, she got out of the birch house and onto the beach. She looked around and saw a boy – Naundyaka. He had harpooned fish and was eating them.

"Naundyaka, who do you live with?" asked Belye.

"I live alone. I have no one," the boy replied.

Belye stayed to live with the boy. She started to hunt, shooting from a bow and arrow – she caught many things. When she went out hunting, she wore men's clothing, and when she came back, she put on her woman's robe. She took care of Naundyaka like a brother.

One day Belye went out hunting as usual. And in this time the brothers came to Naundyaka and started asking questions.

"Who are you living with? Who is sewing for you?"

"I live with my brother," the boy answered.

"How can you have a brother? After all, you were living alone."

Naundyaka never told them. The brothers got angry and broke his toy arrows that Belye had made. He began to cry from the offence of it.

Belye came back from the hunt and asked, "Naundyaka, who has offended you? Who has been here?"

"The brothers Biatu – they wanted to know who I lived with. I said I lived alone. They broke my arrow and went away."

Angry, Belye followed the brothers' tracks. She came to their tent, hooked the door to their hay with her spear, and threw it out into the sea. "Come out, brothers. We will have a contest in shooting with the bow!"

"Who has come to us? Who disturbs the brothers?"

They came out of the hay house. Belye took her special *sasa* earrings from her ears and hung them on a tree.

"The one who can hit a hole in an earring from the bow – that one will prove to be the bravest, with a good aim."

They began with the eldest, then the middle brother, and their arrows flew past. The youngest brother was left, the best shooter with the best aim.

"Show that she does not brag," shouted the eldest. "And how well you shoot!"

The youngest brother shot an arrow from his bow, but the arrow went awry.

Belye took up her bow and let the arrow go. It went right through the hole in the earring, her *sasa*. The brothers were amazed. Belye had beaten them! Belye took her earring from the tree and went away.

She went to the boy Naundyaka. They sat in their birch boat, the *omorochka*, and went to an island. At that time the brothers set off behind them – they wanted to get back at her for their disgrace. They came to Belye's *balagan* and found there was no one there. Then they saw the skin of a black bear on an island, hung by Belye. She and the boy had started to live there. The brothers got on a boat of their own, called a *bat*, and set off to the island. Belye saw them on the way.

"Blow winds, blow powerfully!" she called.

The wind picked up power, the sea raged, and the boat turned over. The brothers all drowned. The wind calmed, and then the water was peaceful. Belye and the boy Naundyaka left the island and returned to their tent on the shore of the sea. They lived peacefully. ▼

5

FOUR SHAMANS

Vasili Ivanovich Dunkai, Victoria Leonidovna Donkan, Vera Semenovna Onenko, Elena Alexandrovna Kilye – How They Changed from the Old to the Present

Before the beginning of shamanism there was an old woman. She was Great Mama, or Sagdy Mama – very old and bent over. In the old woman's time, the cult of the home fire was strong. She is the one who sends the child's soul to the mother. Everything affecting the birth of children was, and still is, with her, while men went on the all-important hunts that brought food.
UDEGE FOLKLORE[1]

Who Are the Shamans?

There is much discussion about when and how shamanic work began. Some say it was at the beginning of the world, and others at an uncertain time later. Many Udege say that women were the first shamans, and would include *Sagdy Mama*, while others insist that she lived before any shamans began to work. These people understood her as a spirit-master who helped babies, children, adults, and elders, in an ancient time. Some say that there were male spirits who were hunters as well. All of this may have been before the name "shaman" appeared in Siberia; it spread later to the Far East.

Shamans, with various names, have lived in places around the world. They have worked as far as Nigeria in Africa, with a name of *juju-man.*[2] We have already stopped using "witch doctor," although some use it. Tuvan shamans use *Kam* for a woman or *Kham* for a man, as do others from North and South America, and beyond. Each have worn their own particular clothes, used different names, and played their own music, much of it drumming.[3] They have had various abilities, depending on their own skills or the needs of their own people.

Specific to the centre of Russia and its Far East, each shaman will do some of the following things, although not necessarily all of them. Accompanying the dead to the next world is the most important for all of them, while divination, seasonal ceremonies, predicting the weather, and mediating disagreements come next. Shamans can show leadership and also give energy healing to a group. Epics and short stories often serve as metaphors for shamans everywhere. Characters often use magic in a story, and travel over impossible distances at great speed. Animals talk. Much of what we have read may have been told for thousands of years – and of course more recently.

Helping people is of most importance to a shaman, but it is also true that people were often frightened by shamans as well as relying on them. This was because their spirits were often connected with death, and the shamans could move away from others when in trance. Shamans have been powerful, and people were careful not to cross them, and for this reason people would often wait to go to a shaman until they were in urgent need.

As odd as it might seem, people would also come out to watch shamans working as a great entertainment. One man explained to me that, after all, they had no television! The shaman might swallow hot coals or be shot in the chest with an arrow, only to come back unharmed.

A shaman will expect to receive an animal or another gift for his work. The size of the gift depends on the family's ability to pay. Families will give the most they can. If they are poor, the shaman is generous and receives very little after working all night, sometimes days or even weeks from home. These distances made things hard for a shaman's wife and children. However, around the years from 1990 to 2000, some did start putting up notices with set fees in Tuva, Buriatia, and the Sakha Republic, and perhaps other places.

Usually, shamans' skills were noticed early in childhood, as soon as they could see things in the future, such as the weather or a grandparent's death or a child's birth – and speak about them. However, under communism, many parents attempted to prevent children from taking up or continuing their practices. Sometimes those who did practise, even very quietly, died under Soviet power. Many were killed in Stalin's purges in the 1930s. Those who did not practise suffered and died from their own illnesses. Some survived secretly, and slowly came back to the public during the 1990s, after the end of Soviet power.

Their initiation includes what is sometimes called the shamanic illness – which is a mystery to medicine. On the other hand, shamans themselves may object to the word "illness." They describe being dismembered by spirits, suffering pain, and even dying. After that, though, the survivors are very powerful and healthy.

There is much discussion about the word "shaman" itself, and where it came from. The Udege and the neighbouring Nanai pronounce the name close to *shama*, with the first sound a cross between the sound "s" and "Sh" – a gentle sound unlike the harder "S" and "Sh" that we may also hear.[4] The sound of "man" at the end of the word shaman emphatically does not indicate gender. The word shaman lives largely in Siberia.

Wherever the shamans came from, they arrived and stayed. Both male and female remained powerful as patriarchy took its place, while women stayed strong as ever, especially around children. At births, mothers were alone in fresh new huts built for giving birth to vitally important little ones. The huts were freshly made for health reasons.

Men were very strong with hunting and fishing – providing food for all. However, we've seen in several stories and in real life that many women also hunt successfully. And men also love their children.

Even more specifically, Udege shamans have been described as either "great" or "small" in their abilities and skills. It is the great shaman *Sagdy sama* (not *Sagdy Mama*) who is able to help the dead to the next world. The great ones sing their *kamlanie*, or shaman's ceremony – and have helpers, both human and spiritual. When a shaman journeys to the lower world, his human helpers hold a belt firmly around him, no matter how much he struggles. It is their job to bring the journeyer back once he has finished. Often the spiritual helpers take the form of wooden spirit figures and use the plant *bagul'nik* – ledum or marsh tea – as well as drums. Music was heard in their ceremonies more than nearly anywhere else in people's lives, and the clothing could be elaborate.

Various musical instruments are played by shamans and by ordinary people too, sometimes at ceremonies. These include numerous sizes of wind instruments, such as flutes made of grasses, whistles of willow, another wind instrument with three holes for notes, as well as a type of trumpet made of tree bark. Jaw harps can be carried anywhere, while their string instruments are larger and played seated. Some have only one string and a bow that is significantly curved.

One of the flutes was played for us in Gvasyugi by Olesia Shamshur. The sound was delicate, and I was surprised to learn how difficult it is, first to make the sound and then to make it accurately in tune. She also danced and played the bells on a shaman's snake-belt. And, of course, there are drums.

It was said that strong shamans could fly while drumming. A "smaller" shaman could take up a drum and heal both himself and other people. But grandmothers and certain other people have magic abilities and work with certain plants without being shamans at all. I have heard that this is sometimes hard for westerners to understand, if they are familiar with shamans in parts of South America where such magic plants are part only of the shaman's work.

People say that shamans from the Kimonko clan, living in the Khor River area, have a special connection with bears, and can connect with what a bear says. I heard twenty years ago about two shamans who went away from the village and fought each other. They never came back. Later, people searched and found two bears that had killed each other, and decided that they were the two shamans.

There are other stories about shamans. I love this one, especially with the addition of Korean history.

The Fisherman Shaman and the Prince

The Nanai storyteller Nikolai Petrovich Beldi was the first to tell this story to me while we waited for his wife, the shaman Mingo Chusanbovna Geiker, who was busy with her shamanic work for someone from Gvasyugi. Nadia had brought a gift and a message from her. This was about 1992 or a bit later. As a storyteller, I have told this story many times after that for many people, children and adults, in Russian and English, and will enjoy doing it again. The words sometimes change, but the idea is still the same.

Long ago there was a shaman who sat by the river every day, fishing. Across on the other side was a prince, with a large army. The prince had a beautiful daughter, and because there were so many soldiers around, he kept her carefully in her own room. From her window she could see the shaman fishing.

Time passed, and one day even her father could notice that her belly was larger. He was furious. "My daughter! Where have you been? Tell me now!"

"Father, I haven't been with anyone," she replied. "Although I did dream of the shaman on the other side of the river."

"That shaman!" her father raged. "I will get rid of him!"

He sent several of his soldiers across the river and they killed the shaman with their swords. The prince was very pleased.

The next morning, both father and daughter looked out their windows. There was the shaman, sitting by the river, fishing.

Again, the prince was furious – even more so than before. This time he sent out his very best soldiers, and they not only killed the shaman – they cut his body into small pieces.

Again, the prince was pleased, and his daughter wept.

And so it went, day after day. Finally, the shaman got sick of it! He called all his people and told them, "There's going to be trouble with this prince. You had better pack up and go north. I will stay here and deal with him, and then I will join you."

The people moved north. Soon after that the prince's soldiers followed after them.

The prince himself came to the shaman and said, "Tell me, what can I do to kill you for once and for all?"

The shaman replied, "You can kill my body, but you will never kill my shamanic power. And you will never kill this little finger." He held the finger out.

Without hesitation, the prince cut off the shaman's little finger. But although the shaman's body died, the finger flew off to the north and turned into a female shaman, who soon arrived with the people and stayed with them.

The soldiers continued on their way, but suddenly a big storm came up – like winter, although it was only August. The soldiers had only summer clothing, and had to turn back. ▼

I had told that story many times when, a couple of years later, I was at a conference in the Sakha Republic in Siberia. It was all about the language and cultures of the Udege and all the Tungus people that run up and down the east. Many of my Udege and Nanai friends who live just north of them were there, since the conference was about their own languages. It was a pleasure to spend time with them when they were not busy with their gardens at home. I also met a Korean woman named Chan Park, a wonderful storyteller with a powerful voice. Strong emotion could be understood clearly without knowing her language. She was eager to join one of our evening tea gatherings. "I have questions," she said.

She told us of an old document, perhaps from the Korean sixteenth century. "There were soldiers who came a long way north into the Nanai lands, but had to turn back because of a freak winter storm in early fall. They left words on a stone telling who they were.

"Has anyone heard about that?" she asked, as we all sipped our tea.

At first no one replied, but then one woman spoke up. "I did hear a story…" She told the same story that I had heard by Nikolai Beldi, with one exception. She included a stone that had been left by the soldiers with writing on it.

"We couldn't read the words, and thought it was Chinese," she said, although admitting that now she couldn't remember exactly where the stone was.

Chan told more at that tea party, but this was the thing we all took away in memory.

Only while writing this book did I learn to what degree Chinese and Koreans had been in Udege territory in the distant past.[5]

History of New Shamans in the Amur Region

In many areas spanning central Siberia, including Tuva, Buriatia, and the Sakha Republic, new, young shamans had been emerging and practising ever since the fall of the Soviet Union in the early 1990s. Siberia and the great Lake Baikal is in the centre of Russia, with about 13 million kilometres of total territory, and it is close to 2,640 kilometres away from Khabarovsk.

The Internet began to come into the cities, but it took a long time to reach the villages. Gvasyugi does not have it even now.

Most shamans claimed they had inherited their abilities. After the collapse of the USSR, they set up village practices and urban clinics, travelling abroad to give workshops. Generally, they have been the focus of much attention, ranging from rabid criticism to cautious acceptance inside their own cultures. Many local people hope to find not only competent healers but strong spiritual leadership. There is also avid interest in shamans from outside the region.

The new shamans' practices have included traditional forms of healing and divination; they also conducted seasonal ceremonies and accompanied the dead. Some also ran less traditional ecotours to sacred places and compiled information from surviving elders.

In the Amur River region however, the few remaining elder shamans were gradually dying out, and no new ones had emerged publicly by 2005. It was difficult to say why. Perhaps the fact that the Indigenous populations are very small had something to do with it. The Slavic population is an overwhelming majority. Perhaps people were still cautious about approaching spiritual matters in public after Soviet communism, and at the same time felt a distaste for the commercialization, commonly seen in larger places. Whatever the reason, there were no more than five living shamans among the more northerly Nanai and Ul'chi people, all elderly. There were none among the Udege, since their last shaman, Adikhini, had died several years before.

Roughly five hundred kilometres north of Khabarovsk, on the Amur River, there lived one person who wondered whether she was a shaman. Her village is Bulava, where the people are the Ul'chi. They speak a Tungus language close to that of Udege and Nanai. For years she was entrusted with valuable information by shamans and other elders of her people who live along the Amur River. She began to visit North America in the mid 1990s, accompanying elder shamans Mingo Geiker and Mikhail Duvan. Later, she began running workshops on her own, helping people to health. All three are now deceased, although Nadezhda Duvan was much younger than the others.

Within a short time, American organizers were calling her a shaman for the sake of popularity, although she herself was modest about it. At the conference in Yakutsk in 2000, she told me very quietly that she was doing "a few things at home," which I think means she was not saying publicly that she was a shaman, and this still seemed not to be recognized by people outside her own village.

She was living primarily in the city of Khabarovsk by then, and only rarely visited the Ul'chi village, a fourteen-hour hydrofoil ride away. Later, however, it was known even in Khabarovsk and beyond that she was practising shamanic healing back in Bulava. Before my 2019 visit, she had died.

Before her death, the venerable Nanai shaman Lindza Beldi of the Naikhin village searched for a student, but did not find a match – someone she wanted to work with and to whom she could entrust her valued knowledge. On the other hand, some young people who felt themselves to have the gift, which could manifest along with an illness, could not find an elder shaman they wanted to learn from – and so they remained untrained and inactive.

One Udege woman became terribly ill when she began to practise skills learned from her shaman grandmother, and she saw that as a reason to quit rather than a reason to go ahead. And a number of people who grew up around practising elder shamans may well have inherited the talent, and yet feel their own calling to be in the performing arts or education instead. These people who grew up around practising elder shamans have much to offer an emerging shaman.

I had never heard this problem of finding a match discussed during my previous twelve years of research in the area, but it makes sense in light of the small native population and the even smaller number of shamans. And now another younger shaman, Nadezhda Duvan, had disappeared.

All this reminded me of the music world, which I have lived in. A match must be found between a teacher and a student or things will simply not work, although those matches may take some time to become comfortable. In some ways, the "match" is as important as finding the right musical instrument. Of course, many people learn without a music teacher, as some do with shamanism.

At last, though, a new shaman emerged, at that point the only one among the Udege. The rest of this chapter will be about recent shamanism, and how it differs from that in the past, as we saw it with Yevdokia Batovna. I start with Vasili Dunkai, a shaman I met for the first time on my earlier trip in 2005.

He was just emerging when several of us first met him in Krasny Yar. By 2019, he was well known in the village and on television and the Internet.

He had students in Khabarovsk and further north, as well as many patients who had been very ill, but now were surprisingly healthy. Unfortunately, he was away when I arrived, but I heard and read a lot about him.

Vasili Ivanovich Dunkai. Still Much Like the Old, but Considered a Foreigner[6]

It was June 2005 when I met the new Udege shaman, Vasili Dunkai, in his home village of Krasny Yar. Friends had seen a special television report devoted to his work and to his consecration – a time of learning based on the work of older shamans that can take anywhere from weeks to months. It ended with a quiet ceremony conducted for relatives and friends by the Buriat shaman Valentin Hagdaev, who had come out from his home near Lake Baikal in the middle of Siberia – more than two thousand kilometres. Everyone was curious about Dunkai, since a new shaman had not emerged for several years.

I was in Russia a bit later for all the excitement, but while there I travelled with Valentina Kyalundzyuga and Lyubov Passar for my first trip to Krasny Yar. The road was almost smooth, much easier than the one we took later. That first time, we had a picnic along the way under big trees, and then emerged from the forest into a glorious field of large yellow lilies. Soon the village appeared. From the car, we saw Dunkai walking on the road, and he agreed to meet later in the day. He was modest when we got to his house, and open about himself. A major issue was his having found initiation outside Krasny Yar. Some saw this as a reason to discount him, and still do, since they feel that all shamans should be local and familiar to the people around, and use the same languages and family shamans. Both Valentina Tunsianovna and Lyubov Passar would like to see a spiritual leader evolve, if possible. I was particularly interested, since I had met the Buriat shaman Valentin Hagdaev when he first was starting on his own shamanic road. Just meeting Dunkai, already it felt like a good match between the two young men.

Dunkai explained that he had suffered for nine years from debilitating headaches. Others had said that he had serious problems with alcohol, which he quietly acknowledged as well. It is a common shamanic illness during initiation, or when a person tries to avoid the shamanic calling. After trying many kinds of treatment with little success, he wound up travelling about six hundred kilometres south to see a Buddhist lama who had come from his home to work in Vladivostok. Already this was outside of tradition on both sides. Buddhism had been present in the centre of Siberia since the eighth century, but not in Vladivostok. It is a port city, where many people mix, and Buddhism did come, probably less than half a century ago. The lama told Dunkai he should practise shamanism and recommended getting in touch with a man named Hagdaev.

Dunkai made the trip to Hagdaev's home by the magnificent Lake Baikal, and the two men found the match they were looking for. Later, Hagdaev came out to Krasny Yar. Dunkai then returned to Irkutsk, near Hagdaev's home, to join a large gathering of shamans. He got busy reading ethnographic works from the nineteenth and early-twentieth centuries and building his healing practice.

Valentina Kyalundzyuga listened to this with a mixture of pleasure and distress. "It's all right to go out and learn from others, but you must do your own," she said, emphasizing how important it would be for him to learn from his own traditions, and also to trust his own instincts. He agreed wholeheartedly, saying he had gone on TV mainly to gain recognition as a real shaman. Again and again, she emphasized that he should do his own work in his own way.

She also feels that it is not a good idea for shamans to meet in large groups, because it brings up bad energies. This was borne out among the Buriat people themselves, just across the lake from Hagdaev's home. Within a few months of a conference and gathering of shamans at Lake Baikal in 1996, two of the shamans died unexpectedly, and the buildings that had been used were burned to the ground. Many Buriats attribute this to the concentration of energies from that gathering.

Problems have also arisen around the shamans' clinics in Tuva, south of Baikal, where shamans work in close quarters. I was allowed to watch once, and was fascinated as a shaman worked with a teenaged girl who was ill. He determined that she must become a shaman herself, and then she would recover. This went well. But since so many people had come to the city and needed their shamans, a building was arranged where one or two shamans would come every week to work. Eventually, it fell apart, since shamans are not used to being so close while working, perhaps because of the spirits.

"The initiation could be done alone," Valentina Tunsianovna said. "People did it in the old days, out in the *taiga*, the quiet mountains full of trees, for as long as they are needed."

This is rarely taken up by others. Today there is more focus on the teaching of shamans than on their finding the gift spontaneously. Recently self-directed initiation has been badly neglected. I suppose this has come about because many young people brought up outside a traditional context have never seen shamans at work, nor have they been taught the many other aspects of traditional culture, including music and storytelling, that surround the shaman's work. That being so, they have been more in need of instruction from those who have had ancestors teaching them.

In 2005, Dunkai's work had two main parts – a healing practice, and work with children, teaching them about their culture. He did distance healing, as well as working with patients who were physically present. During our visit, Valentina consulted him for pain in her shoulders as a kind of test. He worked with her energy, using "non-contact massage," or using his hand a few inches away from the patient, and sometimes a light touch. She felt better as a result. In more serious cases, his healing practice involves drumming as well, which he used extensively in his own healing before beginning to practise with others.

Drums provide our bodies with rhythm, which can bring both calm and excitement. And if the patient is not present, the drumming helps the shaman himself. Generally, the patient is not drumming at that time. Here, Valentina Tunsianovna was able to teach Dunkai complex rhythms that she had learned from elder shamans in her own community when she was a child. Although I don't know the details, the correct drumming can certainly do a lot to help a person get well.

Valentina Tunsianovna and Vasili Dunkai sat talking in a boat on a beautiful day, and we friends swam in the river, wondering what they were talking about. There had been much discussion about shamans when Valentina Tunsianovna was growing up. Interestingly, she said that the shamans she knew had not practised soul retrieval as it is practised widely. In other places, it was said that shamans could fly to find an evil spirit that had taken a soul out of body, possibly dead, or to find the live human who had possessed the spirit of the sick person. It seems to me that the latter may be related to the way we sometimes obsessively think of a person who is bothering us. The shaman then had to take the person back from the effects of the evil spirit.

Valentina says the shaman needs simply to instill a sense of well-being into the patients, who will get better on their own. A sick person could also pray to a *sevekhe*, which are made specifically for the purpose. These are spirit figures, usually made of wood, standing and often exerting their influence in a house. Valentina Tunsianovna once gave me a rather small one, about fifteen centimetres high, when I was leaving to go home. She instructed me to paint blue eyes on the figure when I got there. She says this method was even more direct and very effective at bringing the influence of the figure to life. Other spirit figures are taller.

Self-healing, promoted by shamans, is another thing that seems to be deemphasized by many North Americans, although that may be changing. I have been encouraged to heal myself of serious sunstroke in a desert, and I give energy healings at home to myself and others.

On other occasions, Valentina Tunsianovna has told me about Udege ceremonies to accompany the dead to the next world, which she experienced in childhood. "Accompanying" is the key word. Perhaps an elder had died and he wished to take little Valentina with him, since he was fond of her. Valentina may have become ill. Fortunately, a shaman was at the ceremony, since accompanying the dead was the main focus of traditional shamanic work in the Amur. The shaman worked with the man who had died, so that the child would survive. At last, the man understood that he was dead. Realizing what he was doing, he agreed it was an accident and that he did not want Valentina to die.

I had a similar experience with my own mother when she was near to dying. She could no longer speak well, but it became clear that she assumed that I would go with her. I had to explain firmly that I had a long life still to live and would not go with her just then.

Valentina's story of a person who has died and the shaman who makes sure a beloved one comes back to life after death, reminds me of several ancient stories. One favourite is the Tuvan story of Kang-kys and her father. This is just one part of a long tale.[7]

Apart from Valentina's there are rare mentions in our stories of life after death, with the exception of Yevkokia Kyalundzyuga's "A Shaman Carries the Dead to the Next World" in Chapter 1. It is very common in stories from Tuva. One short section is in "Woman of Steel," bringing it out in a true story.

Woman of Steel – How a Man Came Back to Life

A heroic woman was searching for her parents, who had been taken by enemies years before. At last, she came to a place where two grey-haired women were weeping over a pile of bones.

Both women called to the bones, "Come back to life! Come back to life!"

Kang-kys watched the two women, thinking, "If I ever find my father's bones, this is the way I must bring him back to life."

She spoke to the women. "My name is Kang-kys. I am the daughter to Angyr-Ala and Arbak-Möge. I am looking for my parents."

The two women were amazed. It turned out that one of them was the mother of Kang-kys, and the bones were her father's.

She helped the two women. With careful hands, she gathered the bones and laid them out in the form of a man. Then she poured her entire supply of healing water over the bones, using water from the sacred springs called *arzhaan*. As they watched, the bones began to knit themselves together! And now Kang-kys got up onto her horse, Kara-Kaldar, and leapt over her father's body.

Her father, Arbak-Möge, woke up. "My, what a long time I've slept!" he exclaimed. "And without seeing any dreams!"

He got up and limped off into the steppe-land, calling for his horse. "Ayan-Kula, Ayan-Kula!"

The horse's bones heard the voice of their master. They knit themselves together, they covered themselves with new flesh. Ayan-Kula came running, wiggling his ears for sheer joy. ▾

The tale of Kang-kys is not exactly like Valentina's story, but it opens many doors. Some similar stories are connected with religion – from "Shamanism and the Finnish Kalevala" and "Lemminkäinen to Christianity" – which must mean that people are thinking about life and death deeply.

I was very inspired by Dunkai's work with children in conjunction with the World Wildlife Fund, as they began to understand life, including the practical and the spiritual, human and animal. Their work with the Siberian tiger brought them into the community from Vladivostok to help start a "hunters' school" and stop the poachers from killing the tigers. The children learned not only traditional hunting skills, but also the spiritual practices used by their ancestors when approaching the great *taiga* forest and its inhabitants. We attended a meeting, at which he explained the plan to a group of twenty excited children.

Lyubov Passar was there with us, and pointed out that spiritual values need to come first. Without that, no amount of money can help. Those values are being honoured in Krasny Yar, whose economy depended to a large degree on hunting at that point. Pavel Fomenko of the World Wildlife Fund was present and said he had high hopes for Vasili Dunkai as a spiritual leader. All of them were soon to face the establishment of a national park, which was a subject of much debate in the community. The World Wildlife Fund was clearly more welcome, as it was already in place.[8]

We walked to a little house newly built at the edge of the *taiga*, where hunters could make offerings to the spirits before going out. Although the Udege language is fully understandable in Gvasyugi and Krasny Yar, there are some slight differences. The word for the process in Krasny Yar is *khengki*, sometimes translated as prayer; the Russian is *molitva*. Valentina prefers the word *poklon*, referring to a bow or a worshipful rendering of respect. Of all the Amur peoples, these houses – called *Miol* from the Chinese name – are now used only by the Udege of Krasny Yar. At the moment, Gvasyugi does not have a hut and uses the expression *khengginku bua* – "a place for paying respects." Other Amur peoples also make offerings without a little house.

"The last shaman in Krasny Yar was Nadezhda Martynova," said Dunkai. "She urged people to build a *Miol*, the building itself for worshipful respect."

Dunkai brought others together to build this place to make offerings before hunting. There are three small buildings, for three deities. The main one is *Sansime*, the forest god; next is *Loubaty*, for hunters; finally, there is *Nannyashe*, the one that women turn to. People stop at the buildings to make ceremonies, smudging and leaving gifts. These deities are in Krasny Yar, and may be different in Gvasyugi.

Vasili Dunkai told us a short story passed down from an old hunter, Ivan Geonka, who died in 2013.

"Geonka remembered a friend when he was young who went into the *Miol* and cursed it. He tried to stop his friend, but with no luck. That night the boy's legs puffed up and he was in terrible pain. The shaman came and treated him, and he got over it."

The next day Dunkai took us for a boat trip on the Bikin River. We pulled up on a pebbled point, and Valentina Tunsianovna and Vasili sat in the boat and talked seriously. Although not a shaman, she had grown up participating in frequent shamanic ceremonies and has devoted years to recording and understanding the intricacies of the Udege language and culture. Thus, she was an ideal mentor for this emerging shaman, transmitting information from elder to younger in a time-honoured way. Dunkai was also filling a gap, since the last shaman in Krasny Yar had died twenty years before he began to work. He also admitted that he wanting to be more widely recognized as a shaman.

I haven't seen or heard evidence of the encouragement he had from Valentina Tunsianovna and her advice to go his own way. He went ahead with his friend Valentin Hagdaev, who came there to initiate him later in 2005. This was his own choice. The ceremonies he conducted after that seem to have followed parts of Hagdaev's ways, perhaps mixing a bit of Buddhism as well as the Udege teachings. Some people work with him, and others are against it. As one woman pointed out in 2019, it is largely the people living in his own village that disapprove of his work with Hagdaev. Those living elsewhere are not bothered by that, and they have become his students. It's not that there's anything wrong with Hagdaev, it's just that he may do some things differently, or just that he's from a different place.

People asked how a person becomes a shaman, and Dunkai would say, "It just comes." He had some signs in childhood that he could be a shaman, but no teacher to take him forward in his youth. He had become a shaman at the age of thirty-three and remained an active hunter and fisherman, very athletic and in good shape.

Years have passed, and many people now know about him, coming to his public events, and hearing him on the Internet in towns and cities. He has added healing from the effects of alcohol and drugs to his list of ceremonies for health, along with hunting and education. No one spoke clearly in 2019 about why he had moved to Vladivostok to live, and we did not see him on this trip, although I did hear that he had left his wife in Krasny Yar, and had gone away with another woman. Dunkai also comes from a powerful clan, including those who were active in local politics. I also wonder if his opposition to the national park that came to Krasny Yar had anything to do with his leaving. The park arrived shortly after I had left in 2005.

After the boat trip on the Bikin River, Nadia and I travelled north to meet two shamans, and later one more back in the city. These three are Nanai shamans, and they had varying opinions on Dunkai. Some thought he was brilliant in his teaching, and others had heard of times when his work did not help. It seems each took a particular direction, and no one said anything specific. These three seemed quite different from the shamans who had been working in the 1990s and up to 2005 in my experience, even including Dunkai. This must be because the world they live in has become different so quickly. Two live in small towns, and one in a large city. The small towns are in a different territory than that of the Udege.

Victoria Leonidovna Donkan is actively practising. I had first seen her in Nadia's storytelling contests on the Internet. Vera Semenovna Onenko is not actively practising, but tells about dreams, while Elena Alexandrovna Kilye is more active as a storyteller and artist than as a practising shaman. The latter two were somewhat confusing, which is often the case when one listens to shamans.

In all cases, Nadia and I met with them for conversation, and did not see them in active practice.

Victoria Leonidovna Donkan in Sikachi Alyan – Do Your Own

The sun shone and the wind helped us quickly up the stairs to the museum at Sikachi Alyan, near the village and not far from Khabarovsk. Since 2005, an elaborate building had been built near the famous petroglyphs there, and it is full of information about the ancient stone designs. Other aspects of the village's culture are active, such as the music, dance, and food known by the local people. It's stunning to realize that the designs on the petroglyphs may date to 12,000 BC, and their newer ones to 9000 BC. What amazes me is that many of the embroideries made very recently for clothing and household decoration look very similar to images on the rocks. The river has turned many times, and some of the figures are faint, while the others are still clear.

Inside the building, Victoria Donkan greeted us, and we went down the stairs to where she showed us scenes of how people lived here in the past. Two large rooms are full of historic clothing, boats, dishes, knives, photos, and drawings. She knows the petroglyphs too, full of human faces, elk, swans, and other things hard to discern.

We sat in the largest room. She pointed to an elaborate bridal dress. "The thing about marriage is keeping the way clean," she said. "This dress has coins on it for beauty." As in most of Siberia, coins are seen as beautiful on clothing, and show wealth. On the other hand, Victoria comments on the poor fabric of a robe I had been admiring, and at the same time the beautiful embroidery on it. Certainly, there were times when not even the rich could get good fabric. Embroidery threads may have been kept and become available for the experts. It's also possible that the designs were added later to the dress. Certainly, for a marriage to succeed, things must be kept clean, both physically and spiritually. It's an interesting way of putting it.

Some ancient mirrors were found here too. Made of metal, they are usually simply shiny on one side, with complex decorations on the other. These are rare here in comparison with places in the middle of the continent, where they were used by shamans for divining and for healing. In Tuva, I've heard that a mirror may appear from the air for a novice shaman and then disappear into the sky again when the shaman dies. The mirror sends vibrations, reflecting from mountains and rocks, giving a shaman information. Whether these mirrors were used the same way in the Russian Far East, we do not know, but they seem to hold energy even now.

Victoria is also a language teacher and had recently won an honour for her work. She became a shaman in 2000, realizing it was urgent for her to find a way to do good for others.

"My helping spirits are with me, and they find the way," she says.

And so now she is a shaman, in addition to her other work.

"My ancestors taught me to become one," she said. "And from them I also learned much about the cosmos and spirits. They show me what to do. If you forget your ancestors, you will lose much. Even if you don't remember their names, they will do good for you if you remember. Don't doubt. If you do, those things you are concerned about will get worse. We need to love ourselves in order to take care of our problems and help others with their own.

"All little pains mean something. When you are quiet and relaxed, then you may see what the problem is. You may find that the illness comes from wrong thinking. We all do it – shamans and all. I knew early and saw early. Take good care of the body and it gives good answers. Talking with the spirits brings help.

"Disease comes for a reason. We need cleansing rather than healing. Moving energy is healing, hands and chakras especially. What people do themselves is good, instead of always looking for a healer."[9]

Victoria gave an energy reading for Nadia and one for Alex. However, when I asked, she didn't give me a detailed one, only saying that I am a good person. People never gave me readings years ago when I was in the north either, and they did it only sparingly in Tuva. I'm not sure why. Perhaps it's because I bring different spirits when crossing the ocean? Or is it their innate politeness? Mingo Geiker and Mikhail Duvan were shamans who came to Canada years ago, and I wonder now whether they felt the spirits of our places in the way we do with theirs.

We all sat around Victoria's table, and she closed her eyes. I imagine she simply sees the person's spirit and brings up the question and possible answer.

After this I told her that I have always brought a few small stones from home and set them in various places as an offering. She says this is a way of being good in new places.

Now she talked about shamans and spirits.

"It is good to see a shaman with experience," she said, although she had not had a very good experience with Vasili Dunkai. She didn't explain the problem in detail. "Perhaps two shamans together is not so good," she went on with a laugh. She added that Dunkai's learning had come from a Buriat, and so was not the same as that of shamans from his own territory. Thus, it was believed not to be right. Her own advice was similar to that Valentina Kyalundzyuga had given Dunkai about staying in his own territory.

This is a similar thought expressed by people who had been at the conference at Lake Baikal in 1996 that turned out so dangerously, with death and damage. Victoria says it was not good to have too many together.

I asked about the *Tudin*. I had heard that it was something that Nanai people have, but not the Udege, and wondered why. Nanai people had told me that, in their world, this is a person who could help a shaman, having the ability to see along with him or her internally.

I wanted to confirm that Udege shamans do not have a *Tudin*'s sight, although they do have helpers. The Udege do not see in the same way, seeing only from the outside and not internally. Both Victoria and Nadezhda agreed.

Victoria added something. "There is no need for ritual, no initiation for such a person. A *Tudin* might also become a shaman if asked." True, I hadn't heard of Udege people becoming a shamans in that way, although others may have.

After talking with her, we went out onto the sand and looked at petroglyphs on the large boulders. The ones I remembered from the last visit seemed to be in a different place, reached with more difficulty by boat. We had to climb on a log and cross water, and then clamber on tricky boulders to find the elk petroglyph. Now we were seeing different designs, and this place was an easy walk from the new building. Most of the petroglyphs were much easier to see. It was confusing. Nadia finally explained that the petroglyphs we had seen before were on the other side of a lagoon, and are still hard to get to. This side was much easier to reach, and so the road and the building had been built here. Both places had been washed by the waves for thousands of years. It was exciting to find them all.

Soon after meeting Victoria, Nadia and I set off and got on a bus to go farther north to the village of Naikhin. It took about half the morning to get there, and we were just in time for lunch with some of Nadia's enthusiastic friends before going to see Vera Onenko. As usual, a table was full of fish, salads, and bread, with a sweet cake for dessert. We enjoyed our lovely hostess, Klavdia Andreevna Beldi – not only for her food but also for the magnificent clothing she made, so different from that of the Udege. Though she is well into her eighties, her hand is perfect. In general, Udege women do embroidery that stands up a bit from the fabric, appliquéing a design with fish skin underneath the threads. The Nanai may occasionally do the same, but usually they make an appliqué with no fish skin and simpler designs. Before too long I learned to see the difference clearly.

We also met Raisa Alexeevna Beldi at the meal. Her family name, Beldi, is a very common name among the neighbouring Nanai people, just as

Kimonko is common among the northern Udege. Raisa seemed nervous as we sat down to wait for lunch – making sure to let me know about her status in connection to her work in education. I'm not entirely certain why this bothered me as an introduction, but I was saddened. I had heard she was a storyteller, and so tried to make her more comfortable by asking her to tell a story. That made things worse, and we concentrated on our food.

In the 1990s, I'd meet people over a cup of tea, then admire their embroidery, and then gently ask for a story. They'd say they didn't have one. Nadezhda would start things off by talking about the woman's grandchildren and how well they were doing in her summer camps. And then they would say, "Yes, I've just remembered a story." Those people were from a different generation, and they all remembered many stories, whereas now most don't.

One interesting thing on that day was that I heard about many more storytelling awards in Russia than in Canada, which probably led to us talking about it. Certainly, status is very important in Russia, just as storytellers are in parts of Canada that I live in. There are fewer of them, but of course they do exist.

At last, we all left the table and sat down in the next room to enjoy the embroidery.

Vera Semenovna Onenko – Enigmatic Christian Shaman

After lunch, Nadia and I went up the road to see one of the shamans she admired. Vera Onenko lived just far enough to go by car, although I was dying for a walk by then. The car was provided by a young man who sat waiting, whittling whistles made of reeds. The house was on the top of a hill, looking down over the wide Amur River. Inside we met Vera, who sat with us in a small building beside the house, saying her children were too noisy for us to chat in the house. It was quite chilly, and we all took blankets. Her speech was similar to that of many shamans – enigmatic.

Vera had become a shaman only about five years before, in 2014, but there had been others before her – such as both of her grandparents.

"Even as a child I had flown and seen strange things in my sleep," she began, "and this has continued all my life. I frequently saw a big river appearing with deep meaning which quickly disappeared."

Her grandfather was quiet about what she might do when he was still alive. Many had died for being shamans, killed by the government. After a while, she spoke about the dangers of being shamans in the Soviet period. So many had died or been sent to the terrible prison encampments. Still, under that government Vera herself became a Christian, which seemed odd to me, since Christianity had been as forbidden in some areas as shamanism. However, it returned faster after the fall of Soviet power. It was mainly her connection to both Christianity and shamanism that seemed so unusual to me.

"After the war, my mother went differently," she went on, without explaining what she meant. Vera has memories of childhood – her father was also quiet and never thought that she would take over from her grandparents as a shaman. Finally, some spirits came to Vera, and she stayed quiet about it. But then she had a water spirit that came by the river at night. She told her father about that, and he was surprised and then wondered if she would be a shaman after all.

"At this point, I lost my son," she said. "Feeling I must find him in the other world, I came to my grandmother. We saw two people in a circle above, with unworldly music. I was crying and Grandmother told me I must learn to become a shaman."

After that, Vera saw many things in dreams, still weeping.

"I went to another shaman to ask what to do. Later he told me he would die, and soon he did. He had bad spirits, which, it seemed, would be passed to me as well. My father prayed for me not to become a shaman."

In the Soviet period, everyone had thought it was insane to go that way, and with good reason, since shamans were sent to the camps, where many suffered and died. Even ten or more years after the Soviet period, people were very careful. I saw this everywhere.

"I saw a goddess at that time," she said, again with no explanation. "I am quiet at those times."

She made a point that her shamanistic work was not the only thing she did. As is usual for a woman with a family, she cooked and looked after the children.

"One woman who came to the community turned against me," Vera continued. "I had a drum and had been playing it. Someone saw me with the drum and realized I was a shaman. Many became afraid of me and turned away, so I moved to Sikachi Alyan village, where people would not know me – at least at first. Of course, Grandmother was not afraid of me."

We all knew that only shamans used drums here. And often shamans seemed to be crazy.

"We had a tree and ceremonies at our family place. During the ceremonies, I could see other things, such as unusual colours – like purple skin or green hair. I have seen many people who can become shamans, but it is very challenging, and some have died. Now I can't drum any longer, and have found a lot of connection with Christianity."

Nadia asked if she had helpers as a shaman. "I don't really see them," she replied, "but my father did see them. I was taught by a Buriat, that's why I'm different. I made a belt and sang."

This is interesting, since Buriat shamans like Hagdaev also have helping spirits, although likely different ones from the Nanai.

Vera thinks she needs to be more open with people now if she wants to continue. She is not actively practising shamanism at this time.

On the way out, Nadia told me there are levels of people, and Vera is on one of them. Not the highest one, I think, since she did not mention helping the dead to the next world. Nadia thinks she will be able to do this, and it will be interesting if she decides to continue shamanism along with Christianity.

When we went out, the driver had finished making a delicate flute from a reed.

Elena Alexandrovna Kilye: Artist and Storyteller in a Trance

To see the third shaman, we returned to the city. Elena Kilye lives on the top floor of a building in Khabarovsk, and getting there is a challenge. There is no elevator, and we didn't count the floors. At the top, there is a long hall with no light, and a lot of mysterious things to trip on. It was worth it though, to meet her with our gifts as we have with the others and see her art work, which ranges from paintings to fabric, metal, and numerous interesting oddities on every side. Besides being an artist, Elena is both a shaman and a storyteller, something that fascinates me, since I too am a storyteller, although not a shaman.

For the Udege, there is a kind of story, *ningma*, that comes from a dream or a trance, rather than being based on waking memory or history, which is called *telengu*. The roles of shaman and storyteller may be separate, but they have many of the same skills – especially in Tuva, where the stories are often very long. Professional storytellers everywhere are often in a light trance while performing. On the other hand, a major difference between shamans and storytellers is that people are often frightened of shamans, because of the nature of their spirits, while storytellers are loved for the pleasure of the tales.

Elena sees stories in dreams. In one she heard, "Wherever you live, come to me. Late evening on the edge of sundown is the best time to see a small plant along the water and go from there."

"A 'big shaman,' a '*Tudin*,' and an 'Extrasens' refer to different types of one thing," Elena explained. She agrees with Victoria that a big shaman is the kind who has the ability to help the dead to the next world, and that a *Tudin* is similar to a shaman, but without costume or drum, and can help a shaman. On the other hand, the Russian term "extrasens" is better known in English as a person with telepathy, ESP, or fortune-telling ability.

Elena says that Vasili Dunkai was the first to start her shamanism. She didn't say, but they probably met when he began to become famous, first on TV and the Internet, and later in person, when he worked in Khabarovsk. He told her she was a shaman inside and should make more of it, along with her talent as an artist and storyteller.

But now she keeps quiet, and doesn't really work with it. Instead, she does more with dream work such as this: "I saw people and things as I slept. I went into the trees and a big place opened up, onto a part of the road. I see children who have frozen – I see one of them, but they can't speak."

We drank tea and I gazed at the art.

Here is one of Elena's stories: "The hero Mergen was on shore, shaking from love of the beautiful and intelligent Pudin. He was afraid, and went on growing older, as did Pudin. Both always looked at a particular tree – one with a particular energy. Just watching the tree grow helped him to lose his fear and, as the years went by, they married, and their children grew. They were a good family, all because of the old tree. People lived well and the tree grew well."[10]

Our conversation went on. The phone rang. She came back and told me she had lived in the village of Dada, north of Khabarovsk.

She continued, "That was when the spirits said to me, 'Don't be afraid of us.'"

Elena moves with lots of energy and is very slim. Her home is amazing, at the top of the building, with windows showing the tops of huge trees gently moving as we sip more tea and eat snacks.

Shaman Dunkai had given her a drum. She felt bigger and stronger in trance with the use of the drum. But it has been hard for her to find helpers.

She went on with another story. "What do kids do? Look at these opposites – an elder son is good and the younger one lazy. And they both need to be kind. They go to the mountains and get firewood. The elder one goes up along the river and sees that there's a house with a barn next to it. There are dogs and a girl. He likes her! She invites him and he goes. It's warm, a good feeling with everything clean. She agrees to go with him.

"Meanwhile the younger brother finds a house. It's cold, all bad, the firewood is bad. He thinks, 'Where else can I go?' He agrees to stay.

"Both brothers live."

Most of Elena's stories are short. I can picture them being presented to an audience with art or music. And she's effective in a way we understood only when leaving.

A poem came last – one of her own. She told it quietly, looking us in the eyes.

> From dream comes tradition. It seems endless.
> Just feel. A beautiful picture of becoming a shaman.

Nadia and I find we have been in a trance most of this time with Elena. We try to return to waking reality as we slowly make our way down the many flights of stairs and into the sunny day.

Another Trip

Earlier, when Nadezhda, Alex, and I started out from Gvasyugi to Krasny Yar, it was on a longer trip than the one several years back. This time, the main road was closed and for another we went around to pick up another woman – Oksana and her young son Miron. This road started with a very good freeway but as soon as we turned toward Krasny Yar that changed.

The dirt road got worse and worse, but the hills were beautiful as the sun went down. It felt like a very long day with pleasure and distress. In one place we could look sharply downward through the trees and see a beautiful river flowing and turning, while in several places trees had been cut and were being carried away on trucks. I remembered how people talked about Hyundai when I first visited Krasny Yar in 2005. It was clear then that the severe logging would have destroyed the traditional hunting and fishing, and this could be the same.

6

OKSANA OLEGOVNA ZVIDENNAYA

Politics before and after the National Park

Suddenly our keys would not open the door in the corridor from the outside. A child was alone inside. We were gathered between the kitchen and the corridor to our rooms, all of them on the second floor. Everyone worked at the lock – it had been fine just a short time ago, but not now. Coffee appeared. I had no shoes or coat on and was debating a trip to the outhouse. It was chilly, rainy, and muddy outdoors. Oksana made phone calls and others arrived with tools. No luck. At last, they determined that the child must have accidentally turned the lock from the inside. Oksana called to her son Miron, but he did not come. There was no other entry to the second floor.

After what seemed like forever, a small man took a very rickety ladder outdoors and climbed to a small window in Miron's room. The man had alcohol on his breath, and it made me very nervous to think of him climbing, perhaps breaking the window, and cutting himself. But in a short time, he was in, having entered at the top of the small window. He opened the lock and the door to us. It was as all had thought. The door had been locked accidentally by the child from the inside. This was Udege ingenuity and perseverance at work. Treats came for all, and Miron was happy to see his mother, although he had not cried at all when he was alone.

Oksana Zvidennaya made us welcome to Krasny Yar and brought us to this new building, called the Ethnocultural Centre. Nadia told me before I came that there had been an increase of tourism with the Bikin National Park. People were taking in guests for high prices, whereas in Gvasyugi people still invited us in as guests, and we just brought food and gave gifts, like toys for children or calendars from Canada. When we finally arrived, it turned out that Oksana had arranged things very well. The village felt pleasant, as we were taken to a comfortable place to stay at the large building. Beside the river was a gazebo for picnics, with delicate wood decorations around the roof.

It was raining hard in the whole area when we arrived, and sleep was welcome. The building is made with a large hall on the first floor for events, and with comfortable beds on the second floor for visitors. We had the use of a good kitchen, where both Oksana and Nadia prepared meals – except when we were hosted by other hospitable people in the village. I was allowed to wash dishes only rarely, and snacks could be found at any hour. We looked out the windows through trees to the beauty of the Bikin River rushing over large boulders.

Oksana is a younger friend of Valentina Tunsianovna's, and we had picked her up in the town of Verkhny Pereval, a few hours away on a rough dirt road, enjoying her company on the trip, along with her young son. Now, months later, she has moved fully into Krasny Yar.

She is a social anthropologist and ethnographer, who has been working there on and off during the whole time of the national-park question, and had found out how things worked in Krasny Yar before the park arrived. She has also lived in Moscow and Vladivostok, and prefers Krasny Yar whenever possible. There she acts as a scientific assistant/collaborator while working on a higher degree. Fortunately, she met Pavel Sulyandziga as a leader before he had to leave the country. She knows the history very well, has warm friendships, and sees the benefits that have come with the park.

Krasny Yar and Its Politics, Past and Present

The Udege population was recently about 660 to 690 in Krasny Yar itself, and approximately 1,600 all told. This includes villages and people who have moved away, some to the city. Oksana explained the complexities of the village for me. Some people had moved to what is now Krasny Yar from other local areas. I came to see that Krasny Yar is very different from Gvasyugi, which stayed more unified. Krasny Yar may have had a variety of influences from further places than Gvasyugi, where most have all lived in one place for many years. Oksana may also see other people arriving.

On the other hand, both villages lost much of their own land under the Soviet Union, which was hard on hunters.

Here is one of the long letters that Oksana sent me after I went home.

> Gvasyugi became one of the central places for the Udege in 1930, and Krasny Yar only in 1958. In both cases the Indigenous people lost much of their way of life, although there was an advantage in the fact that the villages got schools with competent and purposeful teachers. Other benefits were living closer together – sharing everything, from stories to the skills of embroidery and woodwork, helping one another. Beside that, most of the younger generations learned the Russian language, as well as mathematics, literature, and more, which could allow them to go on to higher education.
>
> If we look back in history, there were also political reasons for Krasny Yar to grow the way it did – several groups gradually coming together. The unification of nomadic groups into settlements had begun with the advent of Soviet power. In 1933, a school was opened in a camp. In 1936, the Bikin Udege people were united together in a village named Metaheza, where houses, shops, a bathhouse, and a hospital were built for them. But that place flooded, and after a while all the houses were moved to the village of Syain, which is downstream on the Bikin River. It was located near the modern village of Sobolinoe. But there too the village was flooded.
>
> In 1957–58, the village of Krasny Yar was built, where all the Udege people from Metaheza and Syain were finally relocated. This was done primarily to simplify accounting, the work of government agencies, the distribution of aid, and work with the population. It was necessary for them to educate people to live by the new rules. After that, a number of Indigenous people were sent to study as managers in the cities.
>
> This is compared with the people from Gvasyugi, who were gathered from nomads starting as early as the 1920s. The Udege from the Bikin River came later, and were united in the 1930s in the villages of Metaheza, and then Syain, and finally Krasny Yar in 1958.

Of course, the Soviet settlements had made changes in traditional culture, as in other places, and now the education system was perhaps hardest on the children. The introduction of the Russian language was widespread, but that was not all. The main thing was the belittling of traditional culture – transforming it into merely a marginal one. Children became embarrassed by their grandparents or parents if they wore clothes that were not modern. If they spoke the Udege language, dressed skins, sewed traditional clothes, or performed rituals, young people were shy.

The Marxist and other approaches divided society into classes and divided history into developmental levels. Everyone was taught that there are groups of people standing at the highest levels of development, and there are those who are at the lower levels.

This was in all history textbooks.

Of course, the Udege people and other Indigenous peoples of the Amur-Sakhalin region felt that, because of their "lower" origin, they should try to ascend to the "higher" level in any way possible. And before all, they abandoned their culture and imitated the modern system in every possible way. The cult of learning and the prestige of admission to universities was widespread until the 1980s.

Many people proved not to be ready to undertake the necessary initiatives and self-development for the market relations that started to develop in the country. The "*Gromhoz*" or "state management of traditional trading" started collapsing – including jobs such as cutting wood, fishing, hunting. After that the territorial Indigenous commune entitled "Tiger" emerged. Management by a *Gromhoz* model was already familiar to the people. On the other hand, it was not managed by state institutions. Management of a territorial nature was done by local communities.

I first came to Russia in 1993, and I can certainly remember the period when money had gone crazy and changed day by day. The Soviet Union had broken up. People were not paid for their work for months at a time, but they would go to work, just because it was so depressing not to. I remember a woman who decided to sell her car, and by the next day the amount of money she received was just enough to buy a loaf of bread. The people have gone through a lot.

Oksana says that even before the advent of Soviet power, there was already a tendency to form territorial groups. And before the national park in Krasny Yar, there were several ways for people create their politics and work together. Briefly it went like this.

In Krasny Yar, three registered groups had emerged by at least 2010. These groups may be seen as similar to my home province of British Columbia's non-profit groups that help people to find funding and grants through the BC *Societies Act*. For example, I was in an official group named VSOS – "Vancouver Society of Storytelling." For a long time we had benefits, such as reduced fees for the use of performance rooms. In Russia, registrations come via governmental organs – in pension funds, tax funds, etc.

First to develop in Krasny Yar was the commune "Tiger," which represents work, including farming as well as hunting. These people lived in places previously used by their ancestors.

The second, "Dunkai," was led by the shaman Vasili Dunkai with a very small membership. The people did their fishing specifically in the Ussuri River.

The third, "Kyaasa," was run by a single man, E.A Kanchuga, with traditional activities.[1]

All these organizations needed the resources of the *taiga*. All live from the vital forest, hunting and fishing. Almost all women are gatherers, although quite a few of them have been hunters as well.

When I got home, Oksana explained the organizations again, in more detail.

> The three communes, Tiger, Dunkai, and Kyaasa are indeed official and registered. The difference among them is in the form of their organization and the size of the populations.
>
> The two, "Dunkai" and "Kyaasa" are family communes, in principle composed of relatives. They are very small in number, and agree in principle on where they are going. Group decisions are made on their economic questions, such as receiving a quota of fish that members have caught. In the far eastern region, among Indigenous peoples, communities organize to obtain quotas for fish which are caught and distributed among community members and their families.

Efrem Kanchuga was one of those listed, who received fish quotas. Without them he would not have been able to work officially. Efrem Kanchuga was a difficult man, who once stabbed another man, and is still under investigation. He had a rebellious and eccentric character. Therefore, he was prevented from remaining a leader of the community for a long time.

The commune "Tiger" is a "territorial-neighbour" group, an economic organization whose work includes a wide circle of activities. Members may prepare meat and furs, along with gathered resources, such as wood, berries, and ferns. These food items may be placed in in containers. Others may work with ecological and ethnographic tourism, art, or the securing of licences and the development of traditional businesses.

Large numbers of people are involved in these territorial-neighbour groups – this includes representatives of various families who came together simply by living in one territory. Their organization existed before the national park. Now it continues to exist, but its territories are significantly reduced, as are incomes and possibilities.

Since all hunters' benefits have been given to the park, all hunters relocated there too, with a change of land status. There was no other way out. Otherwise, they would not have been allowed to hunt on their own territories.

They become inspectors – a function that comes to them on their own sections of land within the national park. As inspectors they receive a small payment. Only several hunters are not part of the park, and they have parcels of land.

When the park came, new activities emerged with it: ethnographic and ecological tourism, constructing new buildings for activities, including the building where we stayed. Internet was just coming in. The World Wildlife Fund for Nature has given great support to the Udege in all ways, including the park "Bikin."

I have read that Udege people were working for New Year's celebrations, since they now have more equipment to help. A good boat and motor helped the inspectors to look for poachers and keep things in order. Another good Japanese motor carries gas. Four-wheelers to get to the difficult places. All are patrolling to fight poaching.

There have been celebrations such as "Day of the Tiger" and opening the new medical building, and a Post Office.

I've seen great pride in people working in all of these places.

Valentina Tunsianovna is a good friend of Oksana and her son Miron. Most likely she has given them one of her books, and I'm sure they have read this one more than once. The books are very strong and full of women.

Bolongdo. A Woman Hunter. Told by Anna Dzhukenovna Kyalundzyuga in the Years from 1960 to 1980

There lived one Belye by the name of Bolongdo. She went hunting on her own. And what designs she embroidered! Each was different and made with silk thread.

One time, taking her birchbark bucket, she went out for water. While taking up the water, she saw a strand of wool in the ice hole. Such a beauty! Bolongdo took it. Taking up water, she placed the wool into her mouth and wet it with saliva, leading with her lips. She didn't realize that the soul of a baby was in that wool, sent by the father. When she arrived at her tent, she put it in her sewing basket.

After a while, Bolongdo started to notice that her belly was growing. She was surprised. After a while Bolongdo could hardly walk – it became difficult to go for firewood. "What will I do?" she thought. Then she went out of the house and saw – what a wonder! Someone had prepared firewood.

Next it was time to go into the birthing tent. She went to that special place and saw that a new tent had already been made. And the firewood was prepared. As Bolongdo thought, everything was done and ready. She went into the tent and gave birth to a healthy boy.

The time came to return to her own tent, a big and homey place after the smaller birthing tent. Bolongdo thought, "If I had a husband, he would make a cradle." She went into the tent and saw that a cradle had already been made. She laid the child down in it.

Time passed, her son grew big, and he was always running. Bolongdo never stopped thinking, "We'll have to make him skis. If he had a father now, he would be making a child's arrow." Suddenly she heard someone moaning outside.

She ran out of the house and saw Yegdiga, a young man. His arms were all covered in blood. Bolongdo was frightened.

"How did you cut yourself, Yegdiga?"

"I was making an arrow for your son and accidentally cut my arm. Don't worry, Belye. As your son grows, bring him to live with me." Yegdiga spoke and then disappeared.

Bolongdo continued living with her son. She taught him how to hunt with his child's arrow. With that arrow he learned to kill ducks, and his mother fried them on the fire.

Once her son started asking, "Mama, who is my father? What is his name?"

"My son, it is forbidden to ask the name of your father."

"Mama, what kind of name do you have?" Her son persisted.

"My name is Bolongdo," she said, so that her son would calm down.

He ran out of the house. He jumped and flew, repeating his mother's name. "Bolongdo, Bolongdo, Bolongdo!" He jumped and jumped and then fell and forgot his mother's name.

He came to his mother and began saying, "Mama, I forgot your name!"

His mother sat, embroidering designs. Her son was bothering her with his questions. Just so he would stop, she said, "Bolongdo!"

"And what is my father's name?" He wasn't giving up.

"Tsar Gaki," said his mother. Gaki means crow in their language, and it came from Manchuria. Tsar is the leader of our land.

Her son ran out of the house. He jumped and repeated his father's name and his mother's.

"Bolongdo, Tsar Gaki! Bolongdo and Tsar Gaki!"

Then one day Bolongdo set off to find Tsar Gaki, along with her son. They took their things: her sewing basket and his child's arrow – the one made by his father. They walked and walked, and toward evening they came to one ancient woman. She was a very decrepit grandmother, and her hair was white-white, like snow. She had a hunchback and was warming over the fire. Bolongdo bowed to this grandmother and asked for a blessing, and then asked how to find Tsar Gaki.

Her son was playing outdoors, he shot his arrow from the bow. When the arrow fell, he ran after it and shot again. He ran and ran, and lost track of the grandmother's house.

The boy found a path and set off along it. That way he arrived at another house – a very big one. The boy wanted to look in the house. He went in and looked. In the house sat Yegdiga, arrayed in rich clothing.

The boy said, "I got lost. I ran where my arrow fell, and I got here that way."

"Tell me, boy, what is your mother's name," asked Yegdiga.

"My mother is called Bolongdo," said the boy, "and my father is Tsar Gaki."

Yegdiga took the boy in his arms, and from him there came a strong smell of son. The child had searched out his father and soon his mother arrived too. They lived well. ▾

We drove out of Krasny Yar thinking of clever boys and their magical parents. From the window we saw a lot of logging going on, with ash, linden, cedar, and probably more. Alex had heard that the wood would be taken to faraway countries, especially the farther parts of China.

It was hard to say goodbye to the village and to Oksana and Miron back at their own house.

7

ALEXANDER ALEXANDROVICH KANCHUGA

A Wise Man with Good Humour

Alexander Alexandrovich Kanchuga is known as a teacher and keeper of language – both Japanese and Udege. He also gathers folk wisdom, shamanism, and knowledge of the long past, and continues as a storyteller and chronicler of the history of the Bikin Udege. He knows well that life is going on in spite of differences. It is a real pleasure to spend time with this wise man.

He was standing by his fence as we rode through the rain. We stopped and he greeted us. At first, I didn't realize who it was, having been to Krasny Yar only one other time with Valentina Tunsianovna and Lyubov Passar. Valentina and I had stayed a few nights in Alexander Kanchuga's home. He and Valentina Tunsianovna were old friends, dating back to badminton games at the *internat*, or residential school.

I've heard from Pavel Sulyandziga that there was more fighting by Russians than sexual abuse at such schools for the Indigenous people. There was also one big difference with Canada. In Russia, the abuse was among students on the streets, not from teachers in the schools. Anything more serious seems to have happened in other parts of Russia, and in any case many of the students were older. Alexander Alexandrovich and Valentina Tunsianovna were recalling only the good times, if indeed they had ever had any such problems.

There by the fence, he remembered my name and the exact year I had been there. Then I remembered that he had heated up the bath, the *banya*.

What a treat! The room is very hot, there are large containers with water, one hot and another cool. You can put the two together into smaller containers, making just the right temperature. When you are finished washing both hair and body, the water goes onto the floor, where there are small openings to the ground. You come out red and rather relieved to get into the cool evening. We had one in each village on this trip, although not his this time.

Alexander Alexandrovich has a stone figure hanging over the door to keep evil spirits away. In the kitchen, he and others have water from the *kolonko*, an ingenious item that I remembered immediately. I wished we had them in Canada when I was living in the country without piped water – or, for that matter, any Internet. On the wall there's a water container with a small opening on the bottom, often with a mirror above. You can push a little stick that allows a small amount of water to come out for washing hands, teeth, and dishes – and fill it up once in a while from the bucket. It's a good idea to check that there is another container below!

The Japanese Visitor

Alexander talked about a Japanese man who was interested in the Oroch people, since Japanese is close to Oroch and Udege. The man had recently visited, and he told Alexander that he was doing research for his museum in Japan, since some of his ancestors had lived in this territory. Their languages were no longer as close, but some of their relatives were. It would be difficult to find DNA connections definitely now, since some of the families had first come together as long as two thousand years ago. Of course, people may have come together more recently as well.

Alexander always enjoys interesting conversation.

"Long ago there were Japanese and Udege who had a lot of history," he said to us with a twinkle in his eye. "But this man had no story to add. The Udege had more."

I thought of the stories I had read about the Japanese, Korean, Chinese, and Mongolian soldiers who had been on Udege soil during the wars of ancient times, as told by Nadia's family. As we sat, I recalled that it is the distant Tuvans and other Siberians that have the connection with Korean languages, not the Udege, who would belong to a Tungus language group, such as Manchu. Alexander has learned a lot for the benefit of others living in the village.

But now our conversation turned to the appearances of various Udege people. I've certainly noticed how different those people can look, even Nadezhda and Valentina Tunsianovna, who are close relatives. Of course, it can be explained by the many peoples who have come together recently, and those whose families go way back, whether or not they ever had Japanese, Chinese, Korean, and even occasionally Russian languages in their area years ago.[1] It reminds me of Vancouver.

Later, I read that the Chinese had heard of people on the Amur River as early as 770 BC up to 202 BC. There was description of writing by 630 AD. The Chinese took tribute from them. Down through the centuries, there were Korean refugees and later Mongols, Japanese, and Korean colonists. Genghis Khan arrived with much devastation, although much later Valentina's grandfather took the name Genghis (which he pronounced "Chingis") with pride. Through this, people named Jurchen-Udegei had set up agriculture and towns, but it's no surprise that later they moved nomadically into the mountains and forests for long periods. When the Russians appeared in 1644, the people had long experience of other nations.

I also heard from Oksana of the Chinese coming to Primorye much more recently for work or fishing, and most found work gardening. Udege families could have them settle nearby, forming fairly large camps or villages, as in the area where the Kanchuga family had Chinese assistants, who worked in their gardens, keeping small cattle and even horses.

A Linguist and Teacher

Alexander Alexandrovich has great oral cultural memory and a brilliant face – constantly moving from humorous to serious and back in a moment. This man is a linguist, with a great interest in alphabets and sounds – and the way they change. His house is full of books, and I feel at home there.

"I've taught both Russian and Chinese languages in the old school building," he said, "and remember learning from my own childhood. Later I taught to children." Alexander still goes into the school occasionally, to teach children the Udege language. He and Nadia were disturbed that the national park is using English rather than Udege. I pointed out that English is very widespread and useful for tourists, but their point was that Udege is where the people are at the moment. He points out that the woman introducing people there speaks English well enough. I wonder how he feels about Pavel Sulyandziga – whether he either misses his friendship or regrets his leadership. It's possible that he did not want the park; many in the village did not. But others worked hard to make it happen, along with Pavel. And the two may have been warm friends. In the hours of chat, that was not mentioned.

Storytelling will of course be of interest to anyone who spends a lot of time with language and culture – and who has a long-term interest and friendship with Valentina Tunsianovna. The two discuss many things in ancient stories, including about how the world came to be. Certainly, the Udege know many of those stories. Valentina had learned one more while reading the works of early-twentieth-century explorer and topographer, Vladimir Arsenyev, about the ways people come to our world and leave it. It is no surprise to think that long ago people understood the earth they lived on and the sky above – after all, both could be seen. But at that time, they didn't have any idea of a world under the ground. Was there anything after death? All they knew was that there was a terrible monster Gambau-Buin', who simply devoured the dead person. In the end they could be saved by two brothers – Uza and Yegda.

Shamans under the Soviets – and Religions

Conversation turned to shamanism, as it does so often. Alexander began to speak about the shamans in Krasny Yar. At that point I especially wanted to know whether some of them can help the dead to the next world, as so many in the past did. I'd had heard nothing of that so far in this visit, although I had in the past. He wrote a list of local shamans, but many of them are no longer alive.

"Some hid under the Soviets," he said sadly. "I remember one who killed herself when they came to get her." Now his granddaughter says she wants to be one, as do other friends her age. In his usual quick way, he moved from sadness to smiles. For her, it would probably be safer to be a shaman in our world than when he was young. But how will the young learn?

Alexander says that Vasili Dunkai cannot be counted as a real Udege shaman, because his training was largely with a shaman from Buriatia. Certainly, there is a lot of difference of opinion about that. But Alexander Alexandrovich and Valentina Tunsianovna are very definite that shamans need to be "our own."

He has heard that shamanism is the first religion – before Buddhism, Christianity, and Islam. Nadia asked if shamans continued to practise during the Soviet time. He laughed and said that it had to be very carefully done. All the same, he remembered one woman who did –and there were probably more. Indeed, I remember hearing Valentina Tunsianovna saying that, when she was in charge in Gvasyugi, she was required to turn shamans over to the authorities. Instead, she would advise them to go farther down the river for ceremonies, so that the sound could not be heard from the village. There was one woman who darkened her windows for it. Valentina told me this long ago, and I remember her serious face when she said, "After all, they needed the healing."

The shamans that Alexander Alexandrovich has known have dealt with all questions, including those about diseases and animals. He says the shamans could do most things, with the exception of healing cancer, appendicitis, and other modern diseases.

He could have talked much longer, but soon it would be time for us to leave the kind people of Krasny Yar, get back in the car with regret, and at last to go home.

We end with sacred animals, starting with Auntie Dusia and the bear, and end with this story about the relations between tigers and people. It is told all over the tiger's territory, and there are many versions. Here's mine, put together from many I have heard and told. Not all at once – I heard this story in several languages and told it many times, with children and grown-ups. As far as the story goes, Auntie Dusia never mentioned Stalin to me, and her stories of shamanism were told before and after his period. A good story moves every time!

The Boy and the Tiger

A man set out from his home on the shore of Sakhalin Island with his son. The boy was of an age to go on his first real hunting trip away from home – about fourteen.

They went through the *taiga* to the boundaries of their own territory, and there they set up their tent and piled firewood and food outside. They brought soft branches inside to sleep on.

The father now made offerings to spirits of *taiga*, the forest, mountains, and of the four directions. He left food for them, and then cooked up their own supper and ate.

After supper the hunter's son began to boast. "I'm the strongest, the fastest…" and he went on like that. His father was disturbed. "Don't brag, my son. *He* might hear you." Father meant the tiger, Master of the Taiga, a being so revered it is forbidden to call him by name.

The boy ignored his father and went on. "I don't care who it is, animal, human. I can beat them all!"

The father was so disturbed that he wanted to go outside. But when he opened the tent flap, there across the doorway lay a huge tiger! They both stayed inside.

In the night, the father dreamed he was talking with the tiger. "We don't know why you have come here, oh revered one. If you have lost your fire-starter, just tell me, and I will give you mine. If you need precious imported fabrics from China, just tell me – I don't have them with me, but I will bring them to you."

Now at last the tiger replied. "I don't need your goods. What I need is the heart of your son. He has bragged that he is strong and can beat me. I say to you, go home and leave your son here. We will have a competition. If he is stronger, let him kill me, and if I am stronger, I will kill him. If you do not do as I say, I will kill you all."

The father woke up and worried. What could he do? It was a shame to leave his son with a tiger, but he had a wife and other children. If the tiger killed him too, the family could all starve. At last, he got up and very quietly passed the tiger and went home.

His wife came out and said, "Why did you come back so soon? And where is our son?" He didn't want to tell her, but he had to. She said, "It is a shame to leave the boy. But you have done what you had to do."

We will leave them there now and return to the boy in the forest.

The boy was tossing and turning. When he awoke and looked around, his father was gone. He looked outside, and the tiger was still there. The boy was hungry and cold – don't forget that the food and firewood were outdoors. Taking his hatchet, he leapt over the tiger, ran across the clearing, and climbed a tree on the other side, almost to the top, with the tiger nipping at his heels. The tiger climbed, but slipped and got his neck caught between the trunk of the tree and a big branch. He was coughing and choking.

Now the boy felt sorry for the tiger and climbed down – chopping and chopping at the branch until it fell. The tiger fell to the ground and slunk away, coughing and hacking, into the forest.

The boy got down and took food and firewood into the tent and prepared his breakfast.

Looking out again, he saw the tiger – back but not threatening. He seemed to be gesturing to the boy to get up on his back! The boy did, and the tiger took off, up and up through the *taiga* to the very top of the mountain.

A house was there, with poles outside for tying up dogs. On some of them there were tiger skins. The boy got down, and the tiger stood up on his back legs and took off his skin. Underneath, he was a man! He hung his tiger skin on one of the poles.

"Come in." he said. "I want you to meet my parents."

They went in, and there sat an old man and woman. The tiger-man said, "This is my new friend. I was in a bad condition, and this boy could have killed me. But instead, he helped me. I brought him here so that we could give him gifts.

The tiger-man's parents thanked the boy for saving their son's life. They invited him to stay the night, saying they would reward him.

At dinner the father explained, "We are tiger people. We are really people like you, and just put on our tiger skins when we go out among you."

In the night the boy awoke, and the house was rumbling. It was full of tigers, all snoring!

When he awoke in the morning, they were people again, and ate together.

Then the tiger people brought him a big sled filled with sable skins, that beautiful and much-valued fur used for trade and to pay tribute to the Russians.

Before he left, his new friend took him out and taught him many things he needed to know to be a good hunter. How to make traps, how to set them, and how to make a magic circle around the trap so the animals would not know a human had been there.

Before he left, the mother said, "Let us come to an agreement. We will not harm people if they do not harm us first."

The boy agreed, "And we will no longer harm tigers if they do not harm us first."

He got on the sled and rode down the mountain. It was winter now, with snow. Then across the flat land and out onto the shore.

Just imagine how happy his parents were to see him! They had given him up for dead.

Now they traded the sable skins over on the mainland and did very well. As the boy grew up, he became the finest hunter in those parts, and his descendants remained friends with the tiger people. ▼

It is said to be a real sin to hurt a tiger, and Alexander Kanchuga agreed with a heartfelt nod. He added a long story about the bad luck of one person who came to kill a tiger with a gun in order to sell the skin. Bears can also be dangerous, especially in spring, and other animals such as wild boar. All of them can be, when wounded.

Nadia asked about the tiger who doesn't attack if not wounded.

"Tiger and Bear are both in the family of the Udege," Alexander replied. "Our people, at least in the past, did not kill a tiger except if the tiger was wounded. The tigers didn't harm people if people didn't harm them."

As for him, he had seen a mother tiger near his house not long before, walking with her babies on the road.

APPENDIX

Preface

Dr Pavel Sulyandziga is certainly an active and brilliant leader, working now in the United States, as well as in Russia. He has been known as one of the most outspoken Indigenous-rights activists in the Russian federation since the 1980s, as well as an Indigenous-rights activist specifically for the Bikin River. He is a member of the UN Working Group on Business and Human Rights, as well as chairman of the board of the International Development Fund for Indigenous Peoples of the North, Siberia, and the Far East. In 2015, Russian law recognized the Batani Foundation, with Sulyandziga as chair. However, in 2017 the foundation was liquidated by the Russians.

Sulyandziga was also the first vice-president of the Russian Association of Indigenous Peoples of the North (RAIPON) and a member of the United Nations Permanent Forum on Indigenous Issues. He headed the board of the Secretariat of Indigenous Peoples of the Arctic Council and was deputy chairman of the Arctic Council's Sustainable Development Working Group. When Sulyandziga said he would run for president of RAIPON the next year, the Russian Ministry of Justice moved to shut it down.

He received his doctoral degree in economic science and mathematics from Khabarovsk State Pedagogical University. He is now an associate research scholar in Bowdoin College in the United States and worked in a similar way at Dartmouth College.

In 2020, he said, "I have created a non-governmental organization with my colleagues and like-minded people in the United States. It bears almost the same name as the organization that I headed in Russia, and the Russian government first recognized it as a foreign agent and then closed it. Only the word "solidarity" was added the organization in the United States, The International Indigenous Fund for Development and Solidarity Batani. In the language of my people, the Udege, the word "Batani (Bata)" means "boy, or hero."

He meets with American non-governmental organizations, often at Harvard, and with the Indigenous peoples of Maine, in the office of the governor of Maine, and with the University of Maine.

His article, "Parks and Arbitration," was published in the *World Policy Journal* 34, no.4 (Winter 2017/2018) © 2017 World Policy Institute. Thanks to David Stevens, in the name of World Policy, for helping me receive permission on 3 September 2019, to republish this article. (Note: The population mentioned in the article is very likely more by now.)

"Parks and Arbitration"

Bikin National Park is one of very few areas in the Russian Far East that remains untouched by those I consider the "wild barbarians of civilization." It is home to the largest cat on the planet, the Amur tiger, and the Bikin River basin nicknamed "the Russian Amazon." Its forests are known as the lungs of the Northern Hemisphere, just as the Amazon's jungles are in the Southern Hemisphere. The Bikin is also the native land of the Udege people, and about six hundred of us still live there.

The history of Bikin National Park is inseparable from the history of my people, and over the decades the land has been a valuable lens through which to observe the workings of Russian national politics. After years of struggle, in 2015 Bikin became the first national park project in which the government took responsibility for protecting indigenous rights.

My involvement in the fight to defend the Bikin began at the end of the 1980s. At that time, an agreement was signed between the governments of the USSR and South Korea allowing the Seoul-based company Hyundai to rent my people's territory for industrial logging over a thirty-year period. By then only four out of eight Udege groups remained in the region. The four lost groups hadn't been wiped out; they had simply been cut off from their taiga – native home – and were no longer able to engage in traditional activities like hunting and fishing. Some of the tribesmen tried to find happiness in cities; many others relocated to live among their relatives in different Udege populations. These groups – the Namunka, Imanka, Sungariyskaya, and Kuruminskaya – disappeared, although the Imanka are attempting a revival. And all this happened in less than thirty years: Loggers first arrived on their land in the 1960s.

When our territory was handed over to Hyundai, my people immediately resisted. After our struggle gained attention and began to harm the company's image, Hyundai decided to terminate the project. The vice-president of the company even made a "farewell" visit to our Krasny Yar forest, during which he apologized and said that Hyundai had been misled by authorities, and that he did not know the lands were Indigenous when he signed the agreement.

Between 1991 and 2008, the story of the Udege was a story of preservation against development. In those years, my people rebuffed efforts by gold miners, multinational companies, and government agencies to log, mine, and build on our land. We also dealt with other kinds of mistreatment. In 1997, a Malaysian logging company rented Udege lands near the Khor River for fifty years, agreeing to pay the aboriginal people $100,000 in the form of ten vehicles. Even this deal was corrupt – the community received only two vehicles and the remaining eight were given to local authorities. The following year, the governor of the eastern region of Primorsky Krai tried to create a nature preserve in the upper reaches of the Bikin, ostensibly for environmental reasons. But this was just another effort to remove us from our territory. The bylaws of the preserve contained a clause stipulating that we Udege were only allowed to travel to our hunting grounds in the protected area by traditional means of transportation, which prohibited snowmobiles and cars. We sued, and a representative of the governor explained in court that we could use reindeer to move from place to place – even though reindeer had never been bred in that area and the Udege had never ridden them. We lost the suit, but when it became clear to the authorities that we would never stop protesting, they eventually lost interest in the project.

Another example: In 2008, Sergey Darkin, who had been elected governor in 2000, started taking bids on our territory. Seven companies took part in the auction, most of which were affiliated with the governor's business empire. The Udege also participated, with our cost of entry covered by the German environmental ministry under the aegis of cooperation between the United Nations and the World Wildlife Fund. I was a member of the UN Forum on Indigenous Issues at the time, and I met with members of Vladimir Putin's administration to try to persuade them to "influence" the competition. Had we lost, we were prepared to bring international attention to the situation through protests and hunger strikes. After my meetings, the federal government convinced the governor to "give" the territory to the Udege.

I've left out many instances of "smaller" attempts to steal our territory under different pretexts – the development of tourism, beekeeping, or scientific research. These were nearly always accompanied by accusations against the Udege that would justify the seizure of our lands. Opponents claimed we were poachers (who, they said, would ruin the remaining natural areas) and alcoholics (how can we be trusted as managers?) Our struggle against such allegations became its own kind of tradition. Over the years, efforts to coerce us became fiercer and more uncompromising. I was elected chairman of the village council in 1987, and after loggers and representatives of outside industries started showing up, I would often receive offers for bribes and payoffs.

We Udege have always managed to defend our rights and interests, no matter how strong our opponents were, for one simple reason: We are united. When I was first asked decades ago by a young teacher to join the struggle, we spent a long time discussing how to best protect our territory. At the time, I told him that because we did not have much power or money, and there were only about two thousand of us in the entire country, we needed to band together. I spread this idea among my relatives. "If one person protests, they will imprison him. Ten people, a hundred people – they can be imprisoned. But if the entire nation rises up, they will be forced to reckon with our opinions and position." Cohesion was central to our struggle.

The authorities knew this, and on three occasions regional and national officials visited my village while I was away to try to persuade the people to remove me as chairman. It was "explained" to my fellow tribesmen that I had been bought by the loggers and miners, and that I was conducting conversations behind the backs of my own people solely for personal gain.

Each time, the people answered, "Don't worry, we'll deal with this ourselves; his family lives here and when he returns, we'll talk to him. If he's betrayed us as you say, we will throw him in the Bikin River." Things never went further than that.

When I was invited to meet with members of the Putin administration in 2014 to talk about the creation of Bikin National Park, I thought it would be a typically useless pro-forma discussion. The previous year, Putin had signed an order committing to creating the park in order to preserve the Amur tiger. This was done without consulting the Udege, and it seemed clear that the Udege would once again be treated shabbily, and perhaps be kicked off the land. What's more, an international campaign to depict Putin as a champion of the Amur tiger was in full swing. There was a summit for heads of state whose territories contained tigers, a special "Amur Tiger" fund was created, and celebrities, from Leonardo DiCaprio to the Russian pop singer Ilya Lagutenko, lent their support. Lagutenko even attempted to name one of his albums after the Udege term for tiger but used the wrong word entirely.

By that time, politics within the Udege community had dramatically deteriorated. Local Udege leaders, namely the head of the village and the head of village business enterprises, had ceased to speak to their people, preferring to use their power to solve personal problems. The head of business enterprises, after receiving massive amounts of money for various projects – millions of dollars from trading, roughly $1 million in grants from international projects related to the Kyoto Protocols, and around $3 million in revenue from pine-nut production, a major export in the region, took measures that made it impossible to properly document how much he was spending. Those who praised him received funds, while those who tried to investigate him were punished and risked losing their hunting licences and access to resources.

I tried to unite the entire Udege population around resisting the national park, and to start discussions with local authorities, but it quickly became clear that they were too busy deceiving the public. They agreed to my face that it was crucial to organize the people, but behind my back they began writing letters to Kremlin officials, accusing me of having abandoned the Udege. Fearing a conflict with the authorities that could prompt them to cut off services like road maintenance and electricity, the Udege heads of the village and business community joined the governor in a working group about the national park. At that time, I didn't know that at least two businessmen had paid Udege leaders to organize protests against the creation of the national park. Nor did I know that these businessmen were paying journalists to slander Udege leaders to use the territory for their personal aims.

It was under these circumstances that Putin proposed a meeting to discuss the situation in Bikin. When he asked whether it would be possible to work with the Udege on creating a national park, I told him yes, it could happen if certain conditions were fulfilled. After consulting my people, I began to recognize that a national park could allow us to protect our homeland, and would give us the opportunity not just to survive, but to thrive. We decided to form an Udege group to generate the conditions and demands that would protect our rights and people. At the time I doubted the administration would accept our proposals, since they required legislative changes. This was a proposition that I knew from previous experience would be nearly impossible. As a contingency, we discussed the possibility of organizing resistance to the national park if the administration did not meet our conditions.

With the assistance of the Indigenous Peoples Assistance Center and the Amur tiger division of the World Wildlife Fund, we arranged roundtables with ecologists, scientists, and representatives of the Indigenous groups within Russia that had conflicts with existing national parks. After these meetings, our group prepared a package of seven proposals, which we presented to the administration:

1. Guarantee the opportunity to engage in traditional fishing on national park land;
2. Guarantee unhindered access to national park territory for all the inhabitants of the villages within its boundaries, as well as their relatives;
3. Consider any products obtained by Udege hunters on the territory of the national park to be the property of the hunters, who can use them for any purposes, including commercial ones;
4. Create a system of co-management of the national park with Indigenous people;
5. Guarantee jobs at the national park for Indigenous people;

6. Prohibit reduction of the territories of the Udege people under traditional stewardship under any circumstances – though they may be expanded; and
7. Utilize, and take into account without exception, ethnological surveys and expertise in the formation of the national park.

To my surprise, the administration accepted all our conditions with hardly any amendments. Authorities created a working group composed of high-ranking ministers, deputy ministers, and the heads of federal agencies, and I represented the Udege, along with the head of our community. In all my time working with high-ranking Russian officials, I had never before encountered any who kept the promises they made. In this case, they agreed that if our conditions were not met, the park would not be created. It was a rare instance of decency among high-ranking bureaucrats.

As we were working on the arrangement, another group of Udege was busy conducting a smear campaign and engaging in "protests" against the park. The leaders of this group enjoyed the quiet support of local authorities, including high-level intelligence and police officials.

They were involved in all kinds of criminal enterprises with an Udege community business leader. With the help of this man, they were selling the government-determined quota of Udege pine nuts for personal profit. They were covering up an illegal hemp trade on Udege lands, where the plant grows in abundance, and they had received permits to develop tourist resorts on Indigenous lands. Although this eventually became public, none of those involved were ever prosecuted.

Despite the best efforts of those corrupt officials, our work eventually resulted in changes to Russian legislation and, in 2015, the creation of the Bikin National Park. Six of the Udege conditions were wholly fulfilled, and the seventh point – the ethnological survey – was completed with help from the Amur division of the Wildlife Fund.

Right now, two of the national park's three deputy directors are Indigenous. One of these deputy directors is also the chairman of the Council of Indigenous Minorities, an Udege advocacy organization. The park has helped unify the Udege people and has mobilized new initiatives for preserving our culture and traditions. The Parks Department created a division dedicated to the development of traditional Indigenous crafts, while all hunters with plots of land in the Bikin held salaried preservation jobs in the national park. Most importantly, educated Udege youth have begun to return from other parts of the country to work in the park.

The Udege struggle to preserve land in Bikin can be taken as a lesson for other Indigenous peoples about the potential of collaborating with ecologists. It is also a lesson for the next generation of Udege, who will bequeath our native land to their children and grandchildren – just as they received it from us, and just as we received it from our fathers and grandfathers, and they from their ancestors. Alexander Fadeev wrote a book about my people called *The Last of the Udege*, echoing Fenimore Cooper's *Last of the Mohicans*. Both books underline the tragedy of Indigenous peoples' encounters with outside civilizations, yet at the same time they have hope. I'd like to believe that Bikin National Park will also serve as a sign of hope for my people, and the thread of time will not be cut short for the Udege.

GLOSSARY

Words come from the Udege language as spoken in both the northern and southern areas, unless otherwise noted. (R) indicates that the word is Russian; "Krasny Yar" that the word comes from the Udege language as spoken only in the southern area; there are also a few words that are clearly English.

Anbar (R) – A barn
Akhbio-Khualikchi – Kill the goose
Bagul'nik – Ledum plant, often used for smudging in ceremonies
Balagan – A temporary place to live, sometimes a tent
Bat – A kind of boat
Belye – In story, a beautiful, courageous, and intelligent woman
Blage – Spiritual good fortune
Bua – The whole world, or a prayer. See also "Grandmother Bua"
Buhniha – The underworld, under the grave
Dekhené – A sound for singing to help cure a sick child
Dudekhe – A small hill
Dudik – Homemade medicine by Yevdokia Batovna
Emende – The sister of Belye, but she is very awkward and foolish
Enduri – Highest deity
Ene Bayarku – A place called "that crossing"
Ganikhe – Keeper of the water
Gongoi – Drumming

Grandmother Bua – Known as the whole world. See "The Story of the Crow"
Internat (R) – High school
Kadadi – The character of a river full of big boulders
Kamin (R) – Fireplace
Kamlanie – Shaman's singing for a ceremony
Kanda Mafa – A story character, a father who is very difficult for his daughter to deal with
Kava – A small house made of tree bark
Kema – A river located near the water in Primorsky Krai
Khalat (R) – A dress with designs in embroidery
Khengginku – A place for paying respects, also known only in Krasny Yar as Miao, from its Chinese name
Khengki – Prayer. A bow or worshipful rendering of respect
Khuigha – Mythical tree from which babies may come
Khulagi – Red water
Khutakka – The morning star
Kimo/Kema – The name Kimonko was taken from the river Kimo, which is now called Kema
Kolkhoz (R) – Collective farm
Kolonko (R) – Water kept in a kitchen that does not have running water
Kyaasa – A family commune in Krasny Yar
Legenda (R) – A story coming from an oral history
Lemé – A food produced from fat under the skin of a deer, made in the form of a snake, with stripes cut into it
Loubaty – A god, honoured by hunters in Krasny Yar
Lungiye – Master of water
Lydya adman – Master of fire
Mafa-kuti – Tiger in Krasny Yar
Mamasadavan – Mistress of salmon
Manchuria – A large area of land
Mari Binku – The place where people lived before
Mergen, or Merge – An excellent hunter, usually in the Nanai language
Miol – A building for worshipful respect in Krasny Yar, before hunting
Namunka – The sea people
Nanai – Language and people who live near the Udege. Also a village not far north from Khabarovsk

Nannyashe – A god that women turn to. Krasny Yar
Ngasigdai – A musical calling and playing for shamans
Nimanku – A magic story, coming from a dream – waking or sleeping
Obolochku – The skin left after a magical change from crow to man – in the Crow story
Omé – Nest made of skin for children
Omorochka – A birch boat
Poklon (R) – A bow or worshipful rendering of respect
Pudenka – A receptacle made from grasses, representing a person
Sagdi mama – Great-grandmother
Sama begbini – The shaman's face
Sansime – The forest god in Krasny Yar
Sasa – An earring used by Belye
Sazhen (R) – 2.13 metres
Sevekhe – Spirit figures, used by shamans
Shamans – Those to help with lives and dying
Singmu – Mythical snakes that try to catch people and eat them, some living on land and others on water. Known as a crocodile
Tagemu – Clothing
Taiga – Turkic word for a forested mountain, as opposed to a treeless rocky mountain. The word for a rocky mountain in Tuva is Tag.
Telungu – A story from history
Temu – Keeper of the water
"Tiger" – A commune, an economic organization
Tudin – A Nanai person who can help a shaman, having the ability to see along with him or her
Ulu – Slippers
Wood shavings – Used by shamans, and ordinary people for many things, including making babies comfortable in bed
Yegdiga – A story hero, strong and intelligent

NOTES

INTRODUCTION

1 See also Valentina's books in chapter 2.

2 To see the reactions of other Indigenous groups in Russia: "Why Russian's Indigenous People Are Wary of National Parks," from the *New Humanitarian*, 9 May 2017; "Numto Native Reserve in Western Siberian," Nenet and Khanty People UPI, May 2017; IWGIA with Bikin, with Indigenous Udege people, 2 July 2018.

CHAPTER ONE

1 *Taiga*: Turkic word for a forested mountain, as opposed to a treeless rocky mountain.

2 *Merge* is a name for a good hunter, usually in the Nanai language. It is interesting that Antie Dusia uses it, since Yegdiga is the usual name used by the Udege.

3 Arsenev, Орочское сказание, no. 3 (*The Oroch Stories*, no. 3) mostly 75 (1), 76 (2).

4 The *Dudnik* is Angelica plant in Russian, meaning "wild celery." It is used extensively in Korean and Chinese medicine for various purposes. A compound in it may indeed have anti-cancer effects.

5 In this story, the shaman and the child may both be male, although they could easily be female.

6 Wood shavings are used by shamans, and also by ordinary people, for many things, including making babies comfortable in bed.

7 Two words here are familiar among the Edo, or the Benin tribe of Nigeria. *Omé*, meaning living in only one place, and *Udeghe*, meaning a person in a city. I have worked with Comfort Ero, who has helped me with this book as

well as her own. We have learned a great deal – including the nature of shamanism, although in Africa they are not called "shamans." Two of her own books are in the bibliography. Of course, these words may be found in other places around the world.

8 People told me that, during the Second World War, many men lost their lives, and their souls were not taken to the other world by shamans. This is why there were more evil spirits around later.

9 The sound *gongoi* is also the name of the sound of drumming in other parts of the world, including in Edo in Nigeria.

CHAPTER TWO

1 See my earlier book *The Flying Tiger*, 32–3.

2 *Yegdiga* is a common story hero. The name is rarely if ever used for ordinary people.

3 A *sazhen* is 2.13 metres.

4 Comfort Ero, now living in Vancouver, says this story is told in Edo, a part of Nigeria, where it is similar to the tale and character *Asankrueke*.

5 Music. There is a wonderful book about Siberian music, especially Tuvan: *Where Rivers and Mountains Sing: Sound, Music, and Nomadism in Tuva and Beyond*, by Theodore Levin and Valentina Suzukei. Tuvan music is very different from Udege, but it does bring together two or more singing voices with instruments and not the other way around, which is to say, the voices start and then the instruments join in. Another book is by Y.I. Sheikhin. He has a long section with Valentina Kyalundzyuga and M.D. Simonov in their 1998 book, Фольклор Удэгейцев, Ниманку Тэлунгу Ехэ [*Folklore of Udege – Nimanku, Telungu, Yekhe*]. From the series, Memory of Folklore of the Peoples of Siberia and the Far East. Novosibirsk: "Nauka," Siberian Enterprise RAN.

6 For more about shamans and their clothing see chapter 5.

7 This comes up in science as well, and reminds me of hearing years ago about the value of a fallen tree, and why it should be left on the ground. So many beneficial things grow on it.

CHAPTER THREE

1 The park will be looked at in more detail in chapter 4 and others.

2 See chapter 7, in which Valentina Tunsianovna and Alexander Kanchuga talk about their schooling.

3 Another person with two bodies here is in Yevdokia Batovna's story "Sister and Brother."

4 For more detail, see my book *The Flying Tiger*, 18, 32.

5 The full story comes from Arsenyev 1917-125 no. 749–350, under the name Gamby-Buin' (in Russian).

6 Thanks to S.V. Bereznitzkii at The Institute of History, Archeology, and Ethnography of the People of the Far East of Russia. For more of this history, see more translated in English in my book *The Flying Tiger*, 229–305.

7 Legends in Udege are understood as things that really happened, whereas magic tales may have happened in sleep, or in a dream or a shamanic vision. Legends are called *Telengu* and magic tales are *Nimanku* in the Udege language.

8 *Bua* refers to the whole world, and in this case to prayers.

9 For more on Udege, Korean, Japanese, and Chinese connections, see Alexander Kanchuga, chapter 7.

10 See: https://youtu.be/w3rMSTTIQB4-Краевой конкурс сказителей "Нингман" (Первый конкурс) https://youtu.be/tKuNi_6U9E4 - онлайн- трансляция 9 ноября 2018 года. II краевой конкурс сказителей «Нингман». Translated: https://youtu.be/w3rMSTTIQB4 - "Ningman" Regional Storyteller Competition (First Competition) https://youtu.be/tKuNi_6U9E4 - online broadcast 9 November 2018. II regional competition of storytellers "Ningman."

11 Lungiye book. The stories in question are #37, named "Тагэму" ["Tagemu"], and also #69.

12 For other spiritual Masters, see chapter 2 under "What People Believe In."

13 Their book had the financial support of the Ministry of Natural Resources of Khabarovsk Territory. The title is *Мир Хозяина Воды Лунгиэ* [*The World Master of Water*].

CHAPTER FOUR

1 For details, see my book *The Flying Tiger*, 115–16.

2 See chapter 3 for more details about the park.

3 Thanks to David Stevens, in the name of World Policy, for helping me receive permission on 3 September 2019, to use a short piece from "Indigenous Rights Activist from the Bikin River," in *World Policy*, 2017, published online.

4 A longer article, "Parks and Arbitration," can be found in the Appendix.

CHAPTER FIVE

1 Yevdokia Batovna writes more about *Sagdy Mama* in the introduction of Valentina's book on Udege folklore, *Удэгкйскне Ниманку Тэлунгу Ехэ*, 32–3. This is an important text, but probably not available in English. My copy came from a Russian bookstore in New York City many years ago.

2 Comfort Ero, *The Lioness Can Also Roar*, and *The Diary of an African Woman*.

3 See the description of the shaman's robe in Valentina Tunsianovna's museum, chapter 2.

4 More of this history is in chapter 6, with Alexander Kanchuga.

5 I have learned a great deal from Alexander Alexandrovich Kanchuga, Valentina Tunsianovna, and her book.

6 Partially taken from an article first published in *Shaman* 14, nos 1–2 (2006), "Vasili Dunkai, a New Shaman for the Udeghe People." I have added or changed a number of things in 2019.

7 The story is from *Woman of Steel: A Tuvan Epic*, translated and retold by Kira Van Deusen, illustrated by Alexei Sedipkov. A related book is Elias Lönnrot, *The Kalevala: Epic of the Finnish People*. The character related to this one is Lemminkäinen.

8 More information about the Bikin National Park is in chapters 3 and 6.

9 I'm interested in her use of the word *chakra*. Clearly she has found it elsewhere. Besides that, she has some simple and deep ideas in common with Valentina Tunsianovna.

10 *Mergen* and *Pudin* mean the same for the Nanai people as *Yegdiga* and *Belye* do for the Udege.

CHAPTER SIX

1 Efrem Kanchuga is the brother of our friend Alexander Kanchuga, see chapter 7.

CHAPTER SEVEN

1 See History in Nadia's chapter. Also, for more information, see Stephan, *The Russian Far East*, 14–17.

BIBLIOGRAPHY

Balzer, M.M., ed. *Shamanic Worlds: Rituals and Lore of Siberia and Central Asia.* Armonk, NY: M.E. Sharpe, 1997.

Barman, Jean. *Iroquois in the West*. Montreal and Kingston: McGill-Queen's University Press, 2019.

Bloch, Alexia. *Red Ties and Residential Schools: Indigenous Siberians in a Post-Soviet State*. Philadelphia: University of Pennsylvania Press, 2001.

Brezhkov, Dmitry, and Pavel Sulyandziga. "New Report Highlights Indigenous Rights Violations in Russia." Cambridge, MA: Cultural Survival (11 July 2019).

Campbell, Joseph. *Historical Atlas of World Mythology.* Vol. 1: *The Way of the Animal Powers.* New York: Harper and Row, 1988.

Chants chamaniques et quotdiens du bassin d l'Amour [*Shamanic and Daily Songs from the Amur Basin*]. No author listed. Sound recording. Paris: Buda Records, 1997. SDC 95217.

Dunkai, Vasily. "Vasily Dunkai, A New Shaman for the Udeghe People." *Shaman* 14, nos 1–2 (2006).

Ero, Comfort Adesuwa. *The Diary of an African Woman.* Middletown, DE: Author, 2017.

– *The Lioness Can Also Roar.* Vancouver, BC: ASA Books, 2013.

Georg, Stefan, Peter A. Michalove, Alexis Manaster Ramer, and Paul J. Sidwell, "Telling General Linguists about Altaic." *Journal of Linguistics* 34, no. 1 (1999): 65–98.

Grusman, V.M., and A.V. Konovalov. *Between the Worlds: Shamanism of the Peoples of Siberia*. Moscow: Artist and King, 2006.

Halifax, Joan. *Shaman: The Wounded Healer*. London: Thames and Hudson, 1982.

Kendall, Laurel. *The Life and Hard Times of a Korean Shaman*. Honolulu: University of Hawaii Press, 1988.

Kenin-Lopsan, M.B. *Тувинские шаманы* [*Tuvan Shamans*]. Moscow: Transpersonal Institute, 1999.

Kesserman, Karina. "Pavel Sulyandziga: Indigenous Rights Activist, from the Bikin River." *World Policy* (31 May 2017). Available at http://worldpolicy.org/2017/05/31/pavel-sulyandziga-indigenous-rights-activist-from-the-bikin-river/.

Kimonko, Jansi. *Там где бежит Сукпай* [*Where the Sukpai Runs*]. Khabarovsk: Khabarovsk Book Publishers, 1985.

King, Alexander. *Living with Koryak Traditions: Playing with Culture in Siberia*. Lincoln: University of Nebraska Press, 2011.

Kohler, Thomas. *Towards a New Millennium: Ten Years of the Indigenous Movement in Russia*. Document No. 107. Copenhagen: International Work Group for Indigenous Affairs (IWGIA), 2002.

Ksenofontov, G.V. *Легенлы и рассказы о шаманах* [*Legends and Stories about Shamans*]. Irkutsk: np, 1928.

Kyalundzyuga, Valentina. *Два Солнца, Удэгейские Сказки* [*Two Suns: Udege Stories*]. 2nd ed. Khabarovsk: AO Khabarovsk Territorial Typography, 2018.

Kyalundzyuga, Valentina, and M.D. Simonov. *Фольклор Удэгейцев, Ниманку Тэлунгу Ехэ* [*Folklore of Udege – Nimanku, Telungu, Yekhe*]. Memory of Folklore of the Peoples of Siberia and the Far East (series). Novosibirsk: "Nauka," Siberian Enterprise RAN, 1998.

Kyalundzyuga, Valentina, and Nadezhda Kimonko. *Мир хозяаина воды Лунгиэ* [*World of the Master of the Water, Lungiye*]. Khabarovsk: Ministry of Natural Resources, 2016.

Laiz, Álvaro. *The Hunt.* Stockport, England: Lewis Ltd, 2017.

Levin, M.G., L.P. Potapav, and Stephen Porter Dunn. *The Peoples of Siberia*. Institute of Ethnography in the name of N.N. Miklukho Maklaia. Chicago, IL: University of Chicago Press, 1964.

Levin, Theodore, and Valentina Suzukei. *Where Rivers and Mountains Sing: Sound, Music, and Nomadism in Tuva and Beyond.* Bloomington: Indiana University Press, 1996.

Lönnrot, Elias. *The Kalevala. Epic of the Finnish People*. Translated by Eino Friberg. Helsinki: Otava, 1988.

McCall, Sophie, Deanna Reder, David Gaertner, and Gabrielle L'Hirondelle Hill, eds. *Listen Tell: Indigenous Stories from Turtle Island.* Waterloo, ON: Wilfrid Laurier University Press, 2017.

Okladnikov, Alexei. *Ancient Art of the Amur Region*. Leningrad: Aurora Art Publisher, 1981.

Shavkunov, E.V. *Государство Бохай и помятники его культуру в приморье* [*The Bokhai State and Monuments of Its Culture in the Primor'e*]. Leningrad: Nauka, 1968.

Sheikin, Yuri I. *Музыкальные Инструменты и наигрыши* [*Musical Instruments and Playing Them*]. Source unknown.

– *Фольклорная Музыка Удэ, памятники фольклора нородов Сибири и дальнего востока, Ниманку, Телунгу Ехэ* [*Folk Music of the Udege: Monuments of Folklore of the People of Siberia and the Far East, Nimanki, Telungi, and Yekhe*]. Novosibirsk: Nauka, 1998.

Stephan, John J. *The Russian Far East: A History*. Stanford, CA: Stanford University Press, 1994.

Sulyandziga, Pavel. "Indigenous Rights Activist from the Bikin River." *World Policy*, 2017, online. Available at https://jsis.washington.edu/aic/2017/05/31/pavel-sulyandziga-indigenous-rights-activist-from-the-bikin-river/

– "Parks and Arbitration: A Leader of Russia's Udege Community Describes the Decades-long Fight to Create Bikin National Park, the First to Safeguard Indigenous Rights." Native Voices. *World Policy Journal* 34, no. 4 (2017): 6–10. https://read.dukeupress.edu/world-policy-journal/article-abstract/34/4/6/133468/Parks-and-ArbitrationA-leader-of-Russia-s-Udege.

Suzak, Cheryl, Shari M. Huhndorf, Jeanne Perreault, and Jean Barman, eds. *Indigenous Women and Feminism: Politics, Activism, Culture.* Vancouver, BC: UBC Press, 2010.

Tsarev, Vladislav, ed. *Towards a New Millennium: Ten Years of the Indigenous Movement in Russia.* Copenhagen, Denmark: Eks-Skolens Trykkeri Print, 2002.

Vaillant, John. *The Tiger: A True Story of Vengeance and Survival.* New York and Toronto: Alfred A. Knopf, 2010.

Van Deusen, Kira. *Flying Tiger: Women Shamans and Storytellers of the Amur.* Montreal and Kingston: McGill-Queen's University Press, 2001.

– *Kiviuq: An Inuit Hero and His Siberian Cousins.* Montreal and Kingston: McGill-Queen's University Press, 2009.

– *Raven and the Rock: Storytelling in Chukotka.* Seattle and London: University of Washington Press, 1999.

– *Singing Story Healing Drum: Shamans and Storytellers of the Turkic Siberia.* Montreal and Kingston: McGill-Queen's University Press, 2004.

– *Woman of Steel: A Tuvan Epic.* Translated and Retold. Illustrated by Alexei Sedipkov. Vancouver, BC: Udagan Books, 2000.

Zvidennaia, O.O., and N.I. Novika. *Удэгейцы охотники и собриратели реки Бикин етнологическаия экспедциаю* [*Udege, Hunters and Gatherers of the Bikin River. Ethnological expertise*]. Moscow: Strategist, Andrei Iakovlev, 2010.

INDEX